The Art of Project Management: Balancing Time, Budget, and Resources

No part of this publication may be reproduced, distributed, or transmitted in any form or by any means, including photocopying, recording, or other electronic or mechanical methods, without the prior written permission of the publisher, except in the case of brief quotations embodied in critical reviews and certain other noncommercial uses permitted by copyright law.

Copyright © 2024 Infowave MRV
All rights reserved.

Table of Content

Chapter 1: Introduction to Project Management

- o   Overview and significance

Chapter 2: Defining Project Scope

- o   Setting boundaries and objectives

Chapter 3: The Triple Constraint

- o   Understanding time, budget, and resources

Chapter 4: Project Planning Fundamentals

- o   Creating a solid project plan

Chapter 5: Time Management Techniques

- o   Tools and methods for effective scheduling

Chapter 6: Budgeting Basics

- o   Estimating costs and resource allocation

Chapter 7: Resource Management

- Identifying and optimizing resources

Chapter 8: Risk Management

- Identifying, analyzing, and mitigating risks

Chapter 9: Stakeholder Engagement

- Managing expectations and communication

Chapter 10: Project Execution Strategies

- Implementing plans and monitoring progress

Chapter 11: Quality Control in Projects

- Ensuring standards and satisfaction

Chapter 12: Change Management

- Adapting to changes while staying on track

Chapter 13: Performance Measurement

- KPIs and metrics for project success

Chapter 14: Team Dynamics and Leadership

- Building and leading effective teams

Chapter 15: Conflict Resolution

- Navigating disputes and challenges

Chapter 16: Documentation and Reporting

- Keeping records and communicating results

Chapter 17: Tools and Technologies in Project Management

- Software and tools for efficiency

Chapter 18: Case Studies of Successful Projects

- Learning from real-world examples

Chapter 19: Future Trends in Project Management

- Innovations and evolving practices

Chapter 20: Conclusion: The Art of Balancing

- Integrating lessons learned for future projects

Chapter 1: Introduction to Project Management

Project management is a discipline that combines art and science to ensure that projects are completed successfully, on time, and within budget. Whether in construction, IT, marketing, or any other field, the ability to effectively manage projects is crucial for achieving organizational goals and delivering value to stakeholders. In this chapter, we will explore the fundamentals of project management, its significance, key concepts, and the evolving landscape of the field.

What is Project Management?

At its core, project management involves the application of knowledge, skills, tools, and techniques to project activities to meet specific requirements. A project is defined as a temporary endeavor undertaken to create a unique product, service, or result. This temporary nature differentiates projects from ongoing operations, as projects have defined start and end dates, specific objectives, and constraints.

Importance of Project Management

1. **Goal Achievement**: Project management provides a structured approach to defining, planning, and achieving goals. It helps teams

stay focused on project objectives and delivers tangible outcomes.
2. **Resource Optimization**: Effective project management ensures that resources—human, financial, and physical—are used efficiently, minimizing waste and maximizing value.
3. **Risk Management**: Projects are inherently risky. Project management involves identifying potential risks, assessing their impact, and developing strategies to mitigate them. This proactive approach helps avoid setbacks and ensures smoother project execution.
4. **Stakeholder Satisfaction**: By engaging stakeholders and managing their expectations, project managers foster collaboration and enhance satisfaction. This relationship is essential for project success, as stakeholders often influence project outcomes.
5. **Adaptability and Continuous Improvement**: Project management methodologies encourage adaptability. As projects progress, circumstances may change, requiring teams to pivot and make adjustments. This flexibility enables continuous improvement and learning.

Key Concepts in Project Management

1. **The Project Life Cycle**: This encompasses the stages a project goes through from initiation to

closure. It typically includes the following phases:
- **Initiation**: Defining the project and securing approval.
- **Planning**: Developing a detailed plan that outlines how to achieve project objectives.
- **Execution**: Implementing the plan and performing project tasks.
- **Monitoring and Controlling**: Tracking progress, managing changes, and ensuring the project stays on course.
- **Closure**: Finalizing all project activities, delivering outcomes, and closing out the project.

2. **The Triple Constraint**: Often referred to as the project management triangle, this concept highlights the interdependent relationship between time, budget, and scope. Changes in one area will impact the others, and effective project management requires balancing these constraints to achieve project goals.
3. **Project Stakeholders**: Stakeholders are individuals or groups affected by or involved in the project. They include team members, clients, sponsors, and end-users. Understanding stakeholder needs and expectations is critical for project success.
4. **Project Methodologies**: Various methodologies guide project management practices, each with

its strengths and weaknesses. Some popular methodologies include:
- **Waterfall**: A linear approach where each phase must be completed before moving to the next.
- **Agile**: An iterative approach that promotes flexibility and collaboration, often used in software development.
- **Scrum**: A subset of Agile that focuses on delivering work in small, incremental pieces called sprints.

The Evolving Landscape of Project Management

As industries and technologies evolve, so does the practice of project management. The rise of digital tools, remote teams, and globalization has transformed how projects are managed. Project managers now leverage software solutions for collaboration, reporting, and tracking progress in real time. Additionally, the increasing complexity of projects demands that project managers possess not only technical skills but also soft skills, such as communication, negotiation, and emotional intelligence.

Conclusion

Project management is more than a set of processes; it is an essential capability that drives organizational success. By understanding its principles, methodologies, and significance, aspiring project managers can lay a strong foundation for their careers. As we progress through this book, we will delve deeper into the various aspects of project management, equipping you with the knowledge and tools to master the art of balancing time, budget, and resources in your projects.

Chapter 2: Defining Project Scope

Defining the project scope is a critical step in project management that sets the foundation for the entire project. It involves clearly outlining what will be included and excluded from the project, establishing boundaries, and ensuring that all stakeholders have a shared understanding of the project objectives. A well-defined scope helps prevent scope creep, aligns expectations, and serves as a reference point throughout the project lifecycle. In this chapter, we will explore the components of project scope, techniques for defining it, and the importance of effective scope management.

What is Project Scope?

Project scope encompasses all the work required to deliver a product, service, or result. It defines the boundaries of the project, including the specific deliverables, tasks, and milestones necessary to achieve the project objectives. The project scope statement outlines what is included in the project (the "in-scope" items) and what is excluded (the "out-of-scope" items).

Importance of Defining Project Scope

1. **Clarity and Focus**: A clearly defined scope provides direction and focus for the project team. It helps team members understand their

roles and responsibilities and what is expected of them.
2. **Stakeholder Alignment**: Engaging stakeholders during the scope definition process ensures that their needs and expectations are considered. This alignment is crucial for stakeholder satisfaction and project success.
3. **Preventing Scope Creep**: Scope creep refers to the uncontrolled expansion of project scope without corresponding adjustments to time, budget, and resources. A well-defined scope acts as a safeguard against scope creep by establishing clear boundaries.
4. **Resource Management**: Understanding the project scope enables effective resource allocation. By knowing what is required, project managers can identify the necessary resources, estimate costs, and schedule tasks appropriately.
5. **Measuring Success**: A defined scope serves as a benchmark for measuring project success. Once the project is completed, it is easier to evaluate whether the project met its objectives and delivered the expected outcomes.

Components of Project Scope

1. **Project Objectives**: Clearly articulate what the project aims to achieve. Objectives should be specific, measurable, achievable, relevant, and time-bound (SMART).

2. **Deliverables**: Identify the tangible outcomes or products that the project will produce. Each deliverable should be clearly defined, including specifications and acceptance criteria.
3. **In-Scope Items**: List all the tasks, features, and requirements that are included in the project. This section should detail what is explicitly part of the project scope.
4. **Out-of-Scope Items**: Specify what is not included in the project. This helps manage expectations and prevent misunderstandings among stakeholders.
5. **Assumptions and Constraints**: Document any assumptions made during the scope definition process, as well as constraints that may impact the project, such as budget limitations or regulatory requirements.
6. **Stakeholders**: Identify key stakeholders and their roles in the project. Understanding stakeholder interests and influences is essential for effective scope management.

Techniques for Defining Project Scope

1. **Stakeholder Interviews**: Conduct interviews with stakeholders to gather insights into their needs, expectations, and concerns. This qualitative approach helps ensure that the scope aligns with stakeholder priorities.

2. **Work Breakdown Structure (WBS)**: Create a WBS to break the project down into smaller, manageable components. This hierarchical structure helps visualize the project scope and ensures that all deliverables are accounted for.
3. **Requirements Gathering Workshops**: Organize workshops with stakeholders to collaboratively gather requirements and define the project scope. This interactive approach fosters engagement and encourages diverse perspectives.
4. **Surveys and Questionnaires**: Use surveys or questionnaires to collect input from a broader audience. This method can help identify additional requirements and preferences.
5. **Scope Statement**: Develop a formal project scope statement that consolidates all the information gathered during the scope definition process. This document should be clear, concise, and easily understandable.

Managing Project Scope

Effective scope management is an ongoing process that requires continuous monitoring and adjustment. Key practices include:

1. **Regular Scope Reviews**: Conduct periodic reviews of the project scope to ensure it remains aligned with project objectives and stakeholder

needs. This allows for timely identification of any necessary adjustments.
2. **Change Control Process**: Establish a formal change control process to evaluate and manage scope changes. Any proposed changes should be assessed for their impact on time, budget, and resources before approval.
3. **Communication**: Maintain open lines of communication with stakeholders throughout the project. Regular updates and feedback sessions help ensure that everyone is aware of any changes or developments.
4. **Documentation**: Keep thorough documentation of the project scope and any changes made. This provides a historical record that can be referenced later if disputes arise or if lessons need to be learned for future projects.

Conclusion

Defining project scope is a vital step in the project management process that lays the groundwork for successful project execution. By clearly articulating objectives, deliverables, and boundaries, project managers can align stakeholder expectations, prevent scope creep, and optimize resource allocation. As we continue through this book, we will explore how to effectively balance time, budget, and resources, leveraging a well-defined project scope as a key tool for project success.

Chapter 3: The Triple Constraint

In project management, the concept of the triple constraint is fundamental to understanding how projects are executed and managed. The triple constraint, often visualized as a triangle, consists of three key elements: time, budget, and scope. Each of these constraints is interdependent, meaning that a change in one will invariably impact the others. This chapter delves into each component of the triple constraint, their interactions, and the strategies for managing these constraints effectively to achieve project success.

Understanding the Triple Constraint

1. **Time**: This refers to the schedule for the project, including the start and finish dates, milestones, and deadlines. Time management is crucial, as delays can lead to increased costs and stakeholder dissatisfaction. Effective scheduling ensures that all project activities are completed within the designated timeframe.
2. **Budget**: The budget encompasses all financial resources allocated to the project, including costs for labor, materials, equipment, and overhead. Managing the budget is essential to ensure that the project remains financially viable and can deliver the expected value without overspending.

3. **Scope**: As previously discussed, scope defines what is included and excluded in the project. It outlines the specific deliverables, features, and tasks that must be completed to satisfy project objectives. A well-defined scope helps prevent misunderstandings and ensures that all stakeholders are aligned.

The Interrelationships of the Constraints

The triple constraint operates on the principle that any adjustment to one constraint will affect the other two:

- **If you extend the timeline (Time)**, you may need to allocate more resources (Budget) or potentially reduce the project scope (Scope) to meet deadlines.
- **If you increase the budget (Budget)**, you might be able to expedite the project timeline (Time) or enhance the scope (Scope) with additional features or higher-quality deliverables.
- **If you broaden the project scope (Scope)**, you may require more time (Time) to complete the additional work and possibly increase costs (Budget) to accommodate the new requirements.

Understanding these interrelationships is essential for project managers to make informed decisions that align with project goals and stakeholder expectations.

Managing the Triple Constraint

Effective management of the triple constraint involves careful planning, monitoring, and adjustment throughout the project lifecycle. Here are key strategies:

1. **Thorough Planning**: Start with a comprehensive project plan that clearly defines the scope, timeline, and budget. Use tools such as Work Breakdown Structure (WBS) and Gantt charts to visualize the project and facilitate communication among stakeholders.
2. **Stakeholder Engagement**: Involve stakeholders early and often. Their input helps define realistic constraints and ensures alignment on priorities. Regular communication keeps everyone informed and allows for timely feedback.
3. **Prioritization**: Determine which of the three constraints is most critical for the project's success. For example, if time is of the essence, stakeholders may agree to compromise on budget or scope. Conversely, if budget is tight, extending the timeline may be necessary.
4. **Monitoring and Control**: Continuously monitor project progress against the constraints. Use performance metrics to evaluate whether the project is on schedule and within budget. Tools such as Earned Value Management (EVM) can help assess performance.

5. **Change Management**: Establish a formal change control process to evaluate any proposed changes to the project scope, timeline, or budget. Assess the impact of changes on all three constraints before approval.
6. **Flexibility and Adaptability**: Be prepared to adjust plans as new information arises or circumstances change. Flexibility is key to navigating the complexities of project management while keeping the triple constraint in balance.

Real-World Examples

1. **Construction Project**: Consider a construction project where the timeline is tight due to a client's need to occupy the building by a specific date. To meet this deadline, the project manager may choose to increase labor hours (increasing the budget) or streamline some non-critical features (narrowing the scope) to ensure timely completion.
2. **Software Development**: In a software development project, if a new regulatory requirement is introduced after the project has started, this change may require expanding the scope to include additional functionalities. As a result, the project manager might need to request more time to accommodate these changes or additional funding to support the extra work.

Conclusion

The triple constraint is a foundational concept in project management that highlights the delicate balance between time, budget, and scope. Understanding how these elements interact is essential for effective project management. By employing strategic planning, stakeholder engagement, and rigorous monitoring, project managers can navigate the complexities of the triple constraint, ultimately delivering successful projects that meet or exceed stakeholder expectations. As we continue this journey through project management, we will explore further how to implement these strategies in practical scenarios, ensuring that projects are not only completed on time and within budget but also aligned with defined objectives.

Chapter 4: Project Planning Fundamentals

Project planning is a critical phase in the project management lifecycle, serving as the blueprint for successful project execution. A well-structured project plan provides clarity, direction, and a framework for managing time, budget, and resources effectively. In this chapter, we will explore the essential components of project planning, key methodologies, and best practices to ensure a successful planning process.

What is Project Planning?

Project planning involves defining project objectives, determining the necessary activities to achieve those objectives, estimating resources and timeframes, and establishing a comprehensive plan to guide the project team. The goal of project planning is to create a roadmap that aligns the project with stakeholder expectations while ensuring efficient use of resources.

Importance of Project Planning

1. **Clarity and Focus**: A detailed project plan provides a clear understanding of project goals and objectives, ensuring that the project team remains focused on delivering the desired outcomes.

2. **Risk Management**: Planning helps identify potential risks and challenges early in the project. By anticipating these issues, project managers can develop strategies to mitigate risks and respond effectively when they arise.
3. **Resource Allocation**: A well-structured plan allows project managers to allocate resources effectively, ensuring that the right people and materials are available when needed.
4. **Stakeholder Engagement**: Engaging stakeholders in the planning process helps align their expectations with project objectives, fostering collaboration and reducing the likelihood of conflicts later in the project.
5. **Performance Measurement**: A project plan establishes a baseline for measuring progress and performance, making it easier to track milestones and assess whether the project is on schedule and within budget.

Key Components of Project Planning

1. **Project Objectives**: Clearly define the specific objectives the project aims to achieve. Objectives should be SMART (Specific, Measurable, Achievable, Relevant, Time-bound) to ensure clarity and focus.
2. **Scope Definition**: Develop a comprehensive scope statement that outlines what is included and excluded from the project. This includes

deliverables, tasks, and any assumptions made during planning.
3. **Work Breakdown Structure (WBS)**: Create a WBS to break the project down into smaller, manageable components. The WBS helps visualize the project's structure and ensures that all tasks are accounted for.
4. **Schedule Development**: Establish a timeline that outlines when each task will be completed. Tools such as Gantt charts and critical path analysis can help visualize the project schedule and identify dependencies between tasks.
5. **Resource Planning**: Identify the resources required for each task, including personnel, equipment, and materials. Develop a resource allocation plan to ensure that resources are available when needed.
6. **Budgeting**: Estimate the costs associated with each task and develop a comprehensive project budget. Include contingencies for unforeseen expenses and ensure that the budget aligns with project objectives.
7. **Risk Management Plan**: Identify potential risks and develop a risk management plan that outlines how risks will be monitored, assessed, and mitigated throughout the project.
8. **Communication Plan**: Develop a communication plan that outlines how information will be shared among project stakeholders. This includes communication methods, frequency of

updates, and the roles responsible for disseminating information.
9. **Quality Management Plan**: Define the quality standards for the project deliverables and outline the processes for ensuring that quality is maintained throughout the project lifecycle.

Project Planning Methodologies

Several project planning methodologies can guide the planning process. Here are a few popular approaches:

1. **Waterfall**: A linear approach that involves completing each phase of the project before moving to the next. This method is effective for projects with well-defined requirements and minimal changes.
2. **Agile**: An iterative approach that emphasizes flexibility and collaboration. Agile methodologies allow for regular adjustments to the project plan based on stakeholder feedback and evolving requirements.
3. **Scrum**: A subset of Agile that focuses on delivering work in small, incremental pieces known as sprints. Scrum emphasizes collaboration, adaptability, and continuous improvement.
4. **Critical Path Method (CPM)**: A project management technique used to determine the longest sequence of dependent tasks and

calculate the minimum project duration. This helps identify critical tasks that could impact the overall timeline.
5. **PRINCE2 (PRojects IN Controlled Environments)**: A structured project management method that provides a comprehensive framework for managing projects. PRINCE2 emphasizes organization, control, and communication.

Best Practices for Project Planning

1. **Engage Stakeholders**: Involve stakeholders in the planning process to gather insights and ensure alignment with their expectations. This collaboration fosters buy-in and reduces potential conflicts.
2. **Be Realistic**: Set achievable objectives and timelines based on available resources and past experiences. Unrealistic expectations can lead to frustration and project failure.
3. **Document Everything**: Maintain thorough documentation of the project plan, including objectives, scope, schedules, and budgets. This serves as a reference point throughout the project lifecycle.
4. **Monitor and Adjust**: Regularly review the project plan and be prepared to make adjustments as necessary. Continuous

monitoring helps identify potential issues early and allows for timely intervention.
5. **Use Technology**: Leverage project management software and tools to streamline the planning process, enhance collaboration, and improve communication among team members and stakeholders.

Conclusion

Project planning is an essential step in the project management process that lays the groundwork for successful project execution. By clearly defining objectives, developing a comprehensive scope, and outlining resource allocation and timelines, project managers can navigate the complexities of project execution with confidence. As we continue through this book, we will delve deeper into specific aspects of project management, exploring how to effectively balance time, budget, and resources while adhering to the project plan.

Chapter 5: Time Management Techniques

Time management is a crucial skill in project management that directly impacts the success of any project. Efficient time management allows project managers to ensure that tasks are completed within the established timeline, maximizing productivity while minimizing stress. This chapter will explore key time management techniques, tools, and best practices to help project managers effectively plan and control project schedules.

Understanding Time Management in Project Management

Time management in project management involves planning and controlling how much time to spend on specific activities. Effective time management enables project managers to complete projects on time and within budget, while also improving overall efficiency and productivity.

Importance of Time Management

1. **Enhanced Productivity**: Good time management helps project teams work more efficiently, leading to higher productivity levels and quicker project completion.

2. **Reduced Stress**: By effectively managing time, project managers can minimize last-minute rushes and the stress associated with tight deadlines.
3. **Better Decision Making**: Having a clear timeline allows project managers to make informed decisions about resource allocation and task prioritization.
4. **Increased Stakeholder Satisfaction**: Delivering projects on time enhances stakeholder confidence and satisfaction, improving relationships and fostering future collaboration.

Key Time Management Techniques

1. **Setting Clear Objectives**: Establishing clear, measurable objectives is the first step in effective time management. Objectives should be SMART (Specific, Measurable, Achievable, Relevant, Time-bound) to provide clarity and direction.
2. **Creating a Work Breakdown Structure (WBS)**: The WBS is a visual representation that breaks the project down into smaller, manageable tasks. This helps identify all the activities needed to complete the project and provides a clear outline for scheduling.
3. **Developing a Project Schedule**: A detailed project schedule outlines when each task will be completed. Tools like Gantt charts and critical

path method (CPM) help visualize the timeline and identify task dependencies.
    - **Gantt Charts**: These are bar charts that represent the project timeline, showing the start and end dates for each task. Gantt charts provide a clear overview of the project schedule and help identify overlapping tasks.
    - **Critical Path Method (CPM)**: This technique identifies the longest sequence of dependent tasks and determines the minimum project duration. Understanding the critical path helps project managers prioritize tasks that directly impact the project timeline.
4. **Prioritizing Tasks**: Not all tasks are created equal. Use prioritization techniques like the Eisenhower Matrix or MoSCoW method to categorize tasks based on urgency and importance. This helps focus efforts on high-priority tasks that contribute significantly to project success.
5. **Time Blocking**: Allocate specific blocks of time for focused work on particular tasks. This technique helps minimize distractions and enhances productivity by allowing project team members to concentrate on one task at a time.
6. **Setting Deadlines and Milestones**: Establish deadlines for individual tasks and overall project milestones. Milestones are significant points in

the project timeline that indicate progress. Setting these helps motivate the team and provides opportunities to celebrate achievements.
7. **Using Time Tracking Tools**: Utilize time tracking software to monitor how much time is spent on each task. This helps identify inefficiencies and areas for improvement, enabling better time allocation in future projects.
8. **Implementing Agile Time Management**: In Agile projects, time management is approached differently. Agile methodologies emphasize iterative cycles (sprints) and continuous feedback. Time management in Agile involves regularly reassessing priorities and adjusting the schedule based on stakeholder feedback.

Best Practices for Effective Time Management

1. **Regularly Review and Adjust**: Periodically review the project schedule to assess progress and make necessary adjustments. Flexibility is key, as unforeseen circumstances may require changes to the timeline.
2. **Communicate Clearly**: Ensure that all team members are aware of deadlines and expectations. Regular check-ins and status updates help keep everyone aligned and accountable.

3. **Avoid Multitasking**: Multitasking can reduce efficiency and increase errors. Encourage team members to focus on one task at a time to improve overall productivity.
4. **Limit Distractions**: Create a work environment that minimizes distractions. This may include setting aside dedicated work hours, using noise-canceling headphones, or establishing "do not disturb" periods.
5. **Delegate Effectively**: Delegate tasks to team members based on their skills and strengths. Effective delegation ensures that tasks are completed efficiently while allowing project managers to focus on higher-level responsibilities.
6. **Take Breaks**: Encourage team members to take regular breaks to recharge. Short breaks can enhance focus and productivity, preventing burnout and fatigue.
7. **Document Time Estimates**: Keep records of time estimates versus actual time spent on tasks. This helps improve future project planning by providing insights into how long tasks typically take.

Conclusion

Effective time management is a cornerstone of successful project management. By implementing the techniques and best practices outlined in this chapter, project managers can enhance productivity, reduce stress, and ensure that projects are completed on time. As we move forward in this book, we will explore how to integrate time management techniques with other aspects of project management, such as budgeting and resource allocation, to create a comprehensive approach to project success.

Chapter 6: Budgeting Basics

Budgeting is a fundamental aspect of project management that directly impacts the feasibility and success of any project. A well-structured budget provides a financial roadmap for the project, enabling project managers to allocate resources effectively, monitor expenses, and ensure that the project is completed within financial constraints. In this chapter, we will explore the key principles of budgeting, the budgeting process, and best practices for effective budget management.

Understanding Project Budgeting

Project budgeting involves estimating the financial resources required to complete a project successfully. It encompasses all costs associated with project activities, including labor, materials, equipment, overhead, and contingency reserves. A project budget serves as a tool for financial planning, helping stakeholders understand the financial implications of the project and facilitating informed decision-making.

Importance of Budgeting in Project Management

1. **Resource Allocation**: A well-defined budget helps project managers allocate resources effectively, ensuring that the necessary funds are available for each phase of the project.

2. **Financial Control**: Monitoring the budget allows project managers to track expenditures against planned costs, enabling timely identification of any variances and facilitating corrective actions.
3. **Stakeholder Confidence**: A transparent budget instills confidence in stakeholders by demonstrating a clear understanding of financial requirements and a commitment to responsible financial management.
4. **Risk Management**: Budgeting includes provisions for contingencies, allowing project managers to account for potential risks and uncertainties that could impact project costs.
5. **Performance Measurement**: A budget provides a benchmark for measuring project performance, enabling project managers to evaluate whether the project is on track financially.

Key Components of Project Budgeting

1. **Cost Estimation**: The first step in budgeting is estimating the costs associated with each project activity. Cost estimates should be as accurate as possible and can be based on historical data, expert judgment, and market research.
    - **Direct Costs**: These are expenses that can be directly attributed to the project, such as salaries, materials, and equipment.

- **Indirect Costs**: These are overhead expenses that are not directly tied to a specific project activity, such as utilities, administrative salaries, and office supplies.
2. **Contingency Reserves**: A contingency reserve is a budget allocation for unforeseen expenses or risks that may arise during the project. It acts as a financial buffer to absorb unexpected costs, helping to prevent budget overruns.
3. **Funding Sources**: Identify the sources of funding for the project, whether they are internal (company funds) or external (grants, loans, or investors). Understanding funding sources is crucial for managing cash flow and ensuring financial sustainability.
4. **Budget Breakdown**: Organize the budget into categories based on project activities or phases. This breakdown helps stakeholders understand how funds will be allocated and makes it easier to track expenses.
5. **Cash Flow Management**: Effective budget management requires monitoring cash flow to ensure that funds are available when needed. This involves forecasting cash inflows and outflows throughout the project lifecycle.

The Budgeting Process

1. **Define Project Scope**: A clear understanding of the project scope is essential for accurate cost estimation. Ensure that all deliverables, tasks, and resources are defined before estimating costs.
2. **Gather Cost Data**: Collect relevant cost data through research, historical records, and expert consultations. This information serves as the foundation for accurate cost estimates.
3. **Estimate Costs**: Use cost estimation techniques to determine the costs associated with each project activity. Common methods include:
    - **Analogous Estimating**: Using historical data from similar projects to estimate costs.
    - **Parametric Estimating**: Using statistical relationships between historical data and other variables to calculate cost estimates.
    - **Bottom-Up Estimating**: Estimating costs at a granular level for each task and then aggregating them to determine the total project budget.
4. **Develop the Budget**: Create the project budget based on the estimated costs, contingency reserves, and funding sources. Ensure that the budget aligns with project objectives and stakeholder expectations.

5. **Review and Approve**: Present the budget to key stakeholders for review and approval. Address any concerns or questions they may have to gain their support.
6. **Monitor and Control**: Once the budget is approved, implement a system for monitoring expenses against the budget throughout the project lifecycle. Regularly review budget performance and make adjustments as necessary.

Best Practices for Effective Budget Management

1. **Involve Stakeholders**: Engage stakeholders in the budgeting process to gather insights and ensure alignment with their expectations. Their involvement fosters transparency and accountability.
2. **Be Realistic**: Avoid overly optimistic estimates. Consider potential risks and uncertainties when developing the budget to create a more accurate and achievable financial plan.
3. **Document Everything**: Keep thorough documentation of the budgeting process, including assumptions, calculations, and sources of data. This documentation serves as a reference for future projects and aids in auditing.
4. **Use Budgeting Tools**: Leverage project management software and budgeting tools to

streamline the budgeting process and enhance collaboration among team members.
5. **Regularly Review and Update**: Conduct periodic budget reviews to assess performance and make necessary adjustments. This ensures that the budget remains aligned with project goals and reflects any changes in scope or resources.
6. **Educate the Team**: Provide training on budgeting practices for project team members. A well-informed team can contribute more effectively to budget management and help identify potential cost-saving opportunities.

Conclusion

Budgeting is a critical component of project management that requires careful planning, monitoring, and control. By understanding the key principles of budgeting and implementing best practices, project managers can create effective budgets that enhance project success. As we continue through this book, we will explore how to integrate budgeting with other aspects of project management, such as time management and resource allocation, to develop a comprehensive approach to project execution.

Chapter 7: Resource Management

Resource management is a vital aspect of project management that focuses on effectively utilizing various resources—human, financial, material, and technological—to achieve project objectives. Efficient resource management ensures that the right resources are available at the right time, leading to improved productivity, reduced costs, and successful project outcomes. In this chapter, we will explore the fundamentals of resource management, key techniques, and best practices to optimize resource utilization throughout the project lifecycle.

Understanding Resource Management

Resource management involves the planning, allocation, and monitoring of resources to ensure that they are used efficiently and effectively in support of project goals. It encompasses a wide range of resources, including:

1. **Human Resources**: The project team members and stakeholders involved in the project. Effective human resource management focuses on recruiting, training, and retaining skilled personnel.
2. **Financial Resources**: The budget allocated for the project, including costs for labor, materials, equipment, and overhead.

3. **Material Resources**: The physical goods and materials required to complete project tasks, such as construction materials, equipment, and supplies.
4. **Technological Resources**: Tools and technologies that support project execution, including software, hardware, and other technical assets.

Importance of Resource Management

1. **Optimal Utilization**: Effective resource management ensures that resources are allocated and utilized efficiently, maximizing productivity while minimizing waste.
2. **Cost Control**: By managing resources effectively, project managers can avoid over-expenditures and stay within budget, reducing the likelihood of financial issues.
3. **Timely Delivery**: Ensuring that the right resources are available when needed helps maintain project schedules and meet deadlines, enhancing stakeholder satisfaction.
4. **Risk Mitigation**: Proactive resource management helps identify potential resource constraints or shortages, allowing project managers to develop contingency plans to address these risks.
5. **Team Morale and Engagement**: Properly managing human resources fosters a positive

work environment, improving team morale, motivation, and engagement.

Key Components of Resource Management

1. **Resource Planning**: The first step in resource management is to develop a resource plan that outlines the types and quantities of resources required for the project. This includes:
    - Identifying resource needs for each task in the project plan.
    - Estimating the time and effort required for each resource.
    - Determining the availability of resources, including potential constraints.
2. **Resource Allocation**: Once resource needs are identified, allocate resources based on project priorities and team members' skills. This involves:
    - Assigning tasks to team members based on their expertise and availability.
    - Ensuring that material and technological resources are available when needed.
    - Balancing workloads among team members to prevent burnout.
3. **Resource Scheduling**: Develop a schedule that outlines when resources will be needed throughout the project. This includes:
    - Creating timelines for task completion and resource availability.

- - o Utilizing project management tools (e.g., Gantt charts) to visualize resource allocation and scheduling.
  4. **Resource Monitoring and Control**: Continuously monitor resource usage and availability throughout the project lifecycle. This involves:
     - o Tracking progress against the resource plan.
     - o Identifying and addressing any discrepancies or shortages promptly.
     - o Making adjustments as necessary to keep the project on track.
  5. **Performance Evaluation**: Assess the effectiveness of resource management throughout the project. This includes:
     - o Analyzing resource utilization rates and productivity levels.
     - o Collecting feedback from team members about resource availability and support.
     - o Identifying lessons learned for future projects.

Techniques for Effective Resource Management

1. **Resource Leveling**: This technique involves adjusting the project schedule to address resource constraints, such as over-allocating tasks to team members. By redistributing workloads, project managers can prevent burnout and maintain a sustainable pace.

2. **Critical Chain Project Management (CCPM)**: CCPM focuses on managing project constraints and emphasizes the importance of buffer management. By incorporating buffers for resource availability, project managers can address uncertainties and maintain project schedules.
3. **Utilization Rate Tracking**: Monitor the utilization rates of human resources to ensure that team members are neither overworked nor underutilized. Aim for a balanced workload to maintain team morale and productivity.
4. **Resource Pooling**: For projects with shared resources across multiple teams or projects, establish a resource pool that can be accessed as needed. This promotes collaboration and maximizes resource efficiency.
5. **Skill Development and Training**: Invest in ongoing training and skill development for team members to enhance their capabilities. This not only improves resource effectiveness but also fosters team engagement and loyalty.

Best Practices for Resource Management

1. **Engage Stakeholders**: Involve stakeholders in the resource planning process to ensure their expectations are met. Their input can help identify resource needs and priorities.

2. **Communicate Clearly**: Maintain open lines of communication with team members regarding resource allocation and expectations. Regular check-ins can help identify any issues early on.
3. **Use Technology**: Leverage project management software and tools to streamline resource management processes. These tools can assist with tracking resource availability, scheduling, and monitoring performance.
4. **Foster a Collaborative Environment**: Encourage collaboration among team members to share resources and knowledge. A collaborative culture enhances problem-solving and creativity.
5. **Be Flexible**: Be prepared to adapt resource plans as project conditions change. Flexibility allows project managers to respond to unforeseen challenges and opportunities effectively.
6. **Document Lessons Learned**: After project completion, review resource management practices and document lessons learned. This knowledge can be invaluable for improving resource management in future projects.

Conclusion

Resource management is a critical component of project management that ensures the efficient and effective use of various resources. By understanding the principles of resource management and implementing best practices, project managers can optimize resource utilization, control costs, and enhance project success. As we continue through this book, we will explore how resource management interacts with other aspects of project management, including budgeting and time management, to create a comprehensive approach to delivering successful projects.

Chapter 8: Risk Management

Risk management is a critical component of project management that involves identifying, analyzing, and responding to potential risks that could impact the success of a project. Effective risk management allows project managers to minimize the likelihood and impact of negative events while maximizing opportunities for positive outcomes. In this chapter, we will explore the principles of risk management, the risk management process, and best practices for integrating risk management into project planning and execution.

Understanding Risk Management

Risk management refers to the systematic process of identifying, assessing, and prioritizing risks followed by the application of resources to minimize, control, or monitor the impact of those risks. Risks can arise from various sources, including technical issues, financial constraints, regulatory changes, and external factors such as market fluctuations.

Importance of Risk Management

1. **Proactive Approach**: By identifying potential risks early in the project lifecycle, project managers can develop strategies to mitigate their impact, rather than reacting to problems after they occur.

2. **Improved Decision Making**: A structured risk management process provides valuable insights that inform decision-making, helping project managers allocate resources effectively and prioritize tasks.
3. **Enhanced Stakeholder Confidence**: A well-executed risk management plan demonstrates to stakeholders that the project team is prepared for uncertainties, fostering trust and support.
4. **Minimized Financial Losses**: By anticipating and addressing risks, organizations can reduce the likelihood of budget overruns and financial losses, ensuring that projects remain on track.
5. **Increased Project Success**: Effective risk management increases the likelihood of achieving project objectives, contributing to overall project success and stakeholder satisfaction.

The Risk Management Process

The risk management process consists of several key steps:

1. **Risk Identification**: The first step in the risk management process is to identify potential risks that could impact the project. This can be done through various methods, including:

- **Brainstorming Sessions**: Engage team members and stakeholders in discussions to identify possible risks based on their experiences and insights.
- **Checklists**: Use predefined checklists of common risks relevant to similar projects or industries to ensure that no potential risks are overlooked.
- **SWOT Analysis**: Conduct a SWOT (Strengths, Weaknesses, Opportunities, Threats) analysis to identify internal and external factors that could affect the project.

2. **Risk Assessment**: Once risks are identified, assess their potential impact and likelihood of occurrence. This involves:
   - **Qualitative Risk Analysis**: Categorize risks based on their severity and likelihood. Use a risk matrix to prioritize risks as low, medium, or high.
   - **Quantitative Risk Analysis**: For high-priority risks, conduct a quantitative analysis to estimate the potential impact on project objectives, such as cost and schedule.

3. **Risk Response Planning**: Develop strategies to address identified risks based on their priority. Common risk response strategies include:
   - **Avoidance**: Alter project plans to eliminate the risk or its impact.

- **Mitigation**: Implement measures to reduce the likelihood or severity of the risk.
- **Transfer**: Shift the risk to a third party, such as through insurance or subcontracting.
- **Acceptance**: Acknowledge the risk and decide to proceed without taking any action, often used for low-impact risks.

4. **Risk Monitoring and Control**: Continuously monitor identified risks throughout the project lifecycle to assess their status and effectiveness of response strategies. This involves:
   - **Regular Reviews**: Schedule regular risk assessments and updates to the risk register.
   - **Reporting**: Keep stakeholders informed about risks and their status, and adjust response plans as necessary.
5. **Documentation**: Maintain a risk register that documents identified risks, assessment results, response strategies, and monitoring outcomes. This serves as a reference for the project team and helps with future projects.

Risk Management Techniques

1. **Risk Register**: A risk register is a key tool for documenting and tracking risks throughout the project. It typically includes information such as

risk descriptions, assessment results, response strategies, and responsible team members.
2. **Risk Matrix**: A risk matrix is a visual tool that helps prioritize risks based on their likelihood and impact. By plotting risks on the matrix, project managers can quickly identify high-priority risks that require immediate attention.
3. **Scenario Planning**: This technique involves developing potential scenarios based on identified risks and assessing their impacts on the project. Scenario planning helps teams prepare for various outcomes and develop flexible response strategies.
4. **Contingency Planning**: Developing contingency plans for high-priority risks ensures that the project team is prepared to respond quickly if a risk materializes. These plans outline specific actions to be taken, resources required, and responsible team members.
5. **Lessons Learned**: After project completion, conduct a review of the risk management process to identify lessons learned. Document successes and challenges faced in managing risks, and use this knowledge to improve risk management practices in future projects.

Best Practices for Effective Risk Management

1. **Involve the Team**: Engage the project team and stakeholders in the risk management process. Their diverse perspectives can lead to more comprehensive risk identification and assessment.
2. **Be Proactive**: Adopt a proactive approach to risk management by regularly reviewing and updating the risk register throughout the project lifecycle.
3. **Communicate Clearly**: Maintain open lines of communication regarding risks and their status. Ensure that all team members are aware of potential risks and response strategies.
4. **Establish a Risk Culture**: Foster a culture of risk awareness within the project team and organization. Encourage team members to speak up about potential risks and support a collaborative approach to managing them.
5. **Utilize Technology**: Leverage project management software and tools to streamline the risk management process, facilitate communication, and track risks effectively.
6. **Continuously Improve**: Regularly assess and refine risk management practices based on lessons learned and feedback from team members. Continuous improvement enhances the effectiveness of risk management over time.

Conclusion

Risk management is an essential component of project management that enables teams to navigate uncertainties and challenges effectively. By implementing a structured risk management process, project managers can identify potential risks, assess their impact, and develop proactive strategies to mitigate them. As we continue through this book, we will explore how effective risk management integrates with other aspects of project management, such as time, budget, and resource management, to ensure successful project outcomes.

Chapter 9: Stakeholder Engagement

Stakeholder engagement is a vital aspect of project management that involves identifying, analyzing, and actively involving individuals or groups who have an interest in the project. Effective stakeholder engagement fosters collaboration, enhances communication, and ensures that stakeholder expectations are met, leading to successful project outcomes. In this chapter, we will explore the principles of stakeholder engagement, the engagement process, and best practices for managing stakeholder relationships throughout the project lifecycle.

Understanding Stakeholder Engagement

Stakeholder engagement refers to the process of involving stakeholders in project decision-making and activities. Stakeholders can include anyone affected by or having an influence on the project, such as:

1. **Internal Stakeholders**: Team members, project sponsors, management, and other departments within the organization.
2. **External Stakeholders**: Clients, customers, suppliers, regulatory agencies, community members, and other entities outside the organization.

3. **Direct Stakeholders**: Individuals or groups directly impacted by the project outcomes, such as end-users.
4. **Indirect Stakeholders**: Those who may not be directly affected but have an interest in the project's success, such as investors or community leaders.

Importance of Stakeholder Engagement

1. **Enhanced Communication**: Engaging stakeholders fosters open communication, ensuring that everyone is informed and aligned with project goals and progress.
2. **Increased Support**: When stakeholders feel involved in the project, they are more likely to support its objectives, helping to secure necessary resources and approvals.
3. **Better Decision-Making**: Engaging stakeholders brings diverse perspectives and expertise to the decision-making process, leading to more informed and effective outcomes.
4. **Conflict Resolution**: Proactive engagement helps identify potential conflicts early, allowing project managers to address issues before they escalate.
5. **Higher Satisfaction**: Involving stakeholders in the project increases their satisfaction with the outcomes, as they feel their needs and concerns are considered.

The Stakeholder Engagement Process

The stakeholder engagement process consists of several key steps:

1. **Stakeholder Identification**: The first step is to identify all stakeholders associated with the project. This involves:
    - Creating a comprehensive list of individuals and groups with an interest in the project.
    - Categorizing stakeholders based on their influence, interest, and impact on the project.
2. **Stakeholder Analysis**: Once stakeholders are identified, analyze their interests, expectations, and potential influence on the project. This includes:
    - Assessing the level of support or opposition from each stakeholder.
    - Understanding their needs and concerns related to the project.
    - Mapping stakeholders using tools such as the Power/Interest Grid, which categorizes them into four groups: Manage Closely, Keep Satisfied, Monitor, and Inform.
3. **Developing an Engagement Plan**: Create a stakeholder engagement plan that outlines how

to communicate and involve stakeholders throughout the project. This plan should include:
   - Engagement objectives: What you aim to achieve through stakeholder engagement.
   - Communication methods: The channels and formats for communicating with stakeholders (e.g., meetings, emails, reports).
   - Frequency of engagement: How often stakeholders will be updated or involved in project activities.
   - Roles and responsibilities: Clearly define who will be responsible for engaging specific stakeholders.
4. **Implementing the Engagement Plan**: Actively engage stakeholders according to the plan. This may involve:
   - Regular updates and progress reports.
   - Facilitating meetings and workshops to gather feedback and input.
   - Addressing stakeholder concerns and incorporating their feedback into project decisions.
5. **Monitoring and Reviewing Engagement**: Continuously monitor stakeholder engagement efforts and assess their effectiveness. This includes:

- Gathering feedback from stakeholders about their satisfaction with the engagement process.
- Adjusting the engagement plan as necessary to address any changing needs or dynamics.
6. **Documentation**: Keep thorough records of stakeholder interactions, feedback, and engagement outcomes. This documentation serves as a valuable reference for future projects and can help improve engagement practices.

Best Practices for Effective Stakeholder Engagement

1. **Be Transparent**: Maintain transparency in communication to build trust and credibility with stakeholders. Share both successes and challenges openly.
2. **Listen Actively**: Foster an environment where stakeholders feel comfortable expressing their concerns and ideas. Actively listen to their feedback and demonstrate that their input is valued.
3. **Tailor Engagement Approaches**: Recognize that different stakeholders may require different engagement strategies based on their level of influence and interest. Customize communication and involvement methods accordingly.

4. **Engage Early and Often**: Involve stakeholders from the project's inception and maintain regular communication throughout the project lifecycle. Early engagement helps build support and reduces the likelihood of resistance.
5. **Build Relationships**: Focus on building positive relationships with stakeholders by demonstrating empathy, respect, and appreciation for their contributions.
6. **Be Responsive**: Respond promptly to stakeholder inquiries and concerns. Timely communication reinforces the importance of their involvement and fosters a collaborative atmosphere.
7. **Utilize Technology**: Leverage project management software and collaboration tools to facilitate stakeholder communication and engagement. These tools can streamline updates and enhance accessibility.
8. **Evaluate and Adapt**: Regularly assess the effectiveness of stakeholder engagement strategies and make adjustments based on feedback and changing project dynamics.

Conclusion

Stakeholder engagement is a crucial element of project management that significantly impacts project success. By proactively identifying, analyzing, and involving stakeholders, project managers can enhance communication, build support, and ensure that project objectives align with stakeholder expectations. As we continue through this book, we will explore how effective stakeholder engagement interacts with other aspects of project management, including risk management, resource allocation, and project execution, to create a comprehensive approach to achieving successful project outcomes.

Chapter 10: Project Execution Strategies

Project execution is the phase where plans are put into action to achieve project objectives. It involves coordinating people and resources, managing stakeholder expectations, and ensuring that project deliverables are produced according to specifications. Effective project execution strategies are crucial for successful project outcomes. In this chapter, we will explore key strategies for executing projects efficiently and effectively, along with best practices to ensure alignment with project goals.

Understanding Project Execution

Project execution encompasses the processes and activities required to implement the project plan. This phase is where the majority of resources are utilized, and it involves delivering the project's outputs and outcomes. The execution phase includes tasks such as:

1. **Resource Allocation**: Assigning and managing human, financial, and material resources to project tasks.
2. **Task Management**: Ensuring that project activities are completed on time and within budget.

3. **Quality Control**: Monitoring the quality of deliverables to ensure they meet defined standards and requirements.
4. **Communication**: Facilitating effective communication among team members and stakeholders.
5. **Risk Management**: Implementing strategies to mitigate identified risks as they arise during execution.

Importance of Project Execution Strategies

1. **Alignment with Objectives**: Well-defined execution strategies help ensure that project activities align with overall project objectives, leading to successful outcomes.
2. **Resource Optimization**: Effective execution strategies allow project managers to allocate and utilize resources efficiently, minimizing waste and maximizing productivity.
3. **Enhanced Collaboration**: Clear strategies foster collaboration among team members and stakeholders, improving teamwork and communication.
4. **Adaptability**: A flexible execution approach enables project managers to adapt to changes and challenges, ensuring that the project remains on track despite unforeseen circumstances.

5. **Improved Monitoring and Control**: Strategic execution facilitates better monitoring of progress and performance, enabling timely adjustments to keep the project aligned with its goals.

Key Project Execution Strategies

1. **Define Clear Roles and Responsibilities**: Establishing clear roles and responsibilities for team members is essential for effective execution. This involves:
    - Creating a responsibility assignment matrix (RACI) to clarify who is Responsible, Accountable, Consulted, and Informed for each project task.
    - Ensuring that team members understand their roles and how they contribute to overall project success.
2. **Develop a Detailed Work Breakdown Structure (WBS)**: A WBS is a hierarchical decomposition of the project into smaller, manageable components. It helps in:
    - Clarifying project deliverables and tasks.
    - Facilitating accurate resource allocation and scheduling.
    - Enhancing monitoring and reporting by breaking down the project into measurable parts.

3. **Utilize Project Management Tools**: Leverage project management software and tools to facilitate planning, execution, and monitoring. These tools can help with:
    - Task assignment and tracking.
    - Resource allocation and management.
    - Communication and collaboration among team members.
4. **Implement Agile Practices**: Incorporating agile methodologies can enhance project execution, particularly for projects that require flexibility and adaptability. Key agile practices include:
    - **Iterative Development**: Breaking the project into small, manageable iterations or sprints, allowing for frequent assessment and adaptation.
    - **Continuous Feedback**: Engaging stakeholders regularly to gather feedback and adjust project activities based on their input.
5. **Establish Effective Communication Channels**: Communication is critical for successful project execution. Strategies for effective communication include:
    - Setting up regular team meetings to discuss progress, challenges, and next steps.
    - Utilizing collaboration tools (e.g., Slack, Microsoft Teams) for real-time communication and updates.

- Developing a communication plan that outlines the frequency and format of updates to stakeholders.
6. **Monitor Progress and Performance**: Regularly tracking progress against project plans is essential for identifying issues early. This involves:
    - Using key performance indicators (KPIs) to measure project performance.
    - Conducting regular status reports and reviews to assess progress and identify areas for improvement.
7. **Risk Management in Execution**: Continuously monitor and manage risks throughout the execution phase. This includes:
    - Revisiting the risk register regularly to assess the status of identified risks.
    - Implementing risk response strategies as needed and communicating any changes to stakeholders.
8. **Quality Management**: Implement quality assurance and quality control processes to ensure deliverables meet required standards. Key practices include:
    - Developing a quality management plan that outlines quality objectives, metrics, and processes.
    - Conducting regular quality audits and reviews to identify and address any quality issues promptly.

Best Practices for Successful Project Execution

1. **Foster a Positive Team Culture**: Encourage a collaborative and supportive team environment that promotes open communication, trust, and shared goals.
2. **Empower Team Members**: Give team members the authority and autonomy to make decisions related to their tasks. Empowerment fosters ownership and accountability.
3. **Be Adaptable**: Stay flexible and be prepared to adjust plans and strategies in response to changing circumstances or stakeholder feedback.
4. **Celebrate Milestones**: Recognize and celebrate the achievement of project milestones to maintain team motivation and morale.
5. **Document Lessons Learned**: Keep a record of lessons learned during the execution phase. This documentation can inform future projects and improve execution practices over time.
6. **Engage Stakeholders Continuously**: Maintain ongoing communication with stakeholders throughout the execution phase to keep them informed and involved, ensuring their expectations are met.

Conclusion

Effective project execution strategies are essential for turning plans into reality and achieving project success. By defining clear roles, utilizing project management tools, fostering collaboration, and continuously monitoring progress, project managers can enhance execution efficiency and effectiveness. As we continue through this book, we will explore how execution strategies integrate with other aspects of project management, such as risk management, stakeholder engagement, and resource allocation, to create a holistic approach to delivering successful projects.

Chapter 11: Quality Control in Projects

Quality control (QC) is a critical component of project management that focuses on ensuring that project deliverables meet established quality standards and stakeholder expectations. QC involves systematic processes and activities designed to monitor, measure, and improve the quality of project outputs. In this chapter, we will explore the principles of quality control, its importance in project management, key techniques, and best practices for effectively implementing QC in projects.

Understanding Quality Control

Quality control refers to the processes and activities used to ensure that project deliverables are produced to meet specified quality criteria. QC is often confused with quality assurance (QA), but while QA focuses on preventing defects through process design and improvement, QC is primarily concerned with identifying and correcting defects in the final outputs.

Importance of Quality Control

1. **Customer Satisfaction**: Effective QC ensures that products or services meet the expectations and requirements of stakeholders, leading to higher customer satisfaction and loyalty.

2. **Risk Mitigation**: By identifying defects early in the process, QC helps mitigate risks associated with project failures, cost overruns, and reputational damage.
3. **Cost Efficiency**: Addressing quality issues during the execution phase is often less expensive than making corrections after project completion. QC helps prevent costly rework and delays.
4. **Compliance and Standards**: Many industries have regulatory requirements and standards that must be adhered to. QC ensures compliance with these standards, avoiding legal and financial penalties.
5. **Continuous Improvement**: Implementing QC processes encourages a culture of continuous improvement, leading to higher quality outcomes in future projects.

Key Components of Quality Control

1. **Quality Standards**: Establishing clear quality standards is essential for effective QC. These standards should be specific, measurable, and aligned with stakeholder expectations. Common sources for quality standards include:
    - Industry regulations and guidelines.
    - Organizational quality policies.
    - Customer requirements and specifications.

2. **Quality Metrics**: Define metrics to measure quality performance against established standards. Key metrics may include:
    - Defect rates.
    - Customer satisfaction scores.
    - Compliance with specifications.
    - Time to resolve quality issues.
3. **Quality Assurance Plan**: Develop a quality assurance plan that outlines the processes and procedures for monitoring and controlling quality throughout the project lifecycle. This plan should include:
    - Quality control activities and techniques.
    - Roles and responsibilities for quality management.
    - Frequency and methods of quality assessments.
4. **Quality Control Tools and Techniques**: Various tools and techniques can be employed to facilitate effective quality control. Some commonly used methods include:
    - **Checklists**: Use checklists to verify that all quality requirements have been met before deliverables are finalized.
    - **Inspections**: Conduct regular inspections of work products to identify defects and ensure compliance with quality standards.

- **Testing**: Implement testing procedures to evaluate the functionality and performance of deliverables.
- **Statistical Process Control (SPC)**: Utilize SPC techniques to monitor processes and identify variations that may indicate quality issues.
5. **Quality Audits**: Conduct regular quality audits to assess the effectiveness of QC processes and identify areas for improvement. Audits can help ensure that quality standards are being followed and that corrective actions are taken when necessary.

The Quality Control Process

The quality control process typically involves the following steps:

1. **Planning**: Develop a quality control plan that outlines the quality standards, metrics, and processes to be used throughout the project.
2. **Execution**: Implement quality control activities according to the quality control plan. This includes conducting inspections, tests, and audits as necessary.
3. **Monitoring**: Continuously monitor quality performance by collecting data on quality metrics and analyzing results. This helps identify any deviations from quality standards.

4. **Evaluation**: Assess the results of quality control activities to determine whether deliverables meet established standards. If quality issues are identified, take corrective actions to address them.
5. **Reporting**: Document and report on quality control findings, including the status of quality metrics, identified issues, and corrective actions taken. Share this information with stakeholders to maintain transparency.
6. **Continuous Improvement**: Use lessons learned from the quality control process to refine quality standards and processes for future projects. Encourage a culture of continuous improvement among team members.

Best Practices for Effective Quality Control

1. **Involve Stakeholders**: Engage stakeholders in the development of quality standards and metrics to ensure that their expectations are clearly understood and met.
2. **Foster a Quality Culture**: Promote a culture of quality within the project team by emphasizing the importance of quality and encouraging team members to take ownership of quality outcomes.
3. **Train Team Members**: Provide training and resources to team members to enhance their understanding of quality control processes and

techniques. Empower them to identify and address quality issues proactively.
4. **Utilize Technology**: Leverage project management software and quality control tools to streamline quality monitoring and reporting processes. Automation can improve efficiency and accuracy in quality control.
5. **Establish Clear Communication**: Maintain open communication about quality expectations and performance. Ensure that team members feel comfortable discussing quality concerns and suggesting improvements.
6. **Perform Root Cause Analysis**: When quality issues arise, conduct root cause analysis to identify the underlying causes of defects. This approach helps prevent recurrence and promotes continuous improvement.
7. **Document Processes and Findings**: Keep thorough documentation of quality control processes, findings, and corrective actions. This documentation serves as a valuable reference for future projects and helps maintain consistency in quality practices.

Conclusion

Quality control is an essential component of project management that ensures deliverables meet established quality standards and stakeholder expectations. By implementing effective quality control processes, project managers can mitigate risks, enhance customer satisfaction, and foster a culture of continuous improvement. As we continue through this book, we will explore how quality control integrates with other aspects of project management, such as risk management, stakeholder engagement, and project execution, to create a comprehensive approach to achieving successful project outcomes.

Chapter 12: Change Management in Projects

Change is an inevitable part of any project. Whether driven by evolving stakeholder requirements, unforeseen circumstances, or improvements in processes, managing change effectively is crucial for project success. Change management involves a structured approach to transitioning individuals, teams, and organizations from a current state to a desired future state. In this chapter, we will explore the principles of change management, the change management process, key strategies, and best practices for successfully managing change in projects.

Understanding Change Management

Change management refers to the process of preparing, supporting, and helping individuals and teams to make organizational changes. It involves understanding the impact of change, managing resistance, and ensuring that changes are implemented smoothly and successfully.

Key Aspects of Change Management:

1. **Identifying Change**: Recognizing when a change is necessary or beneficial to the project.

2. **Assessing Impact**: Evaluating how the change will affect project objectives, stakeholders, and processes.
3. **Planning for Change**: Developing a structured plan for implementing the change, including communication and training.
4. **Implementing Change**: Executing the change management plan, ensuring that all stakeholders are engaged and informed.
5. **Monitoring and Reinforcing Change**: Tracking the progress of the change implementation and reinforcing the new behaviors and processes.

Importance of Change Management

1. **Minimizes Resistance**: Proper change management helps to minimize resistance from stakeholders and team members by involving them in the process and addressing their concerns.
2. **Increases Engagement**: Engaging stakeholders in the change process fosters ownership and commitment, increasing the likelihood of successful implementation.
3. **Ensures Clarity**: A well-structured change management approach provides clear communication about the reasons for the change, its benefits, and its impact.
4. **Improves Project Outcomes**: Effective change management helps ensure that changes align

with project objectives and enhance the overall success of the project.
5. **Facilitates Continuous Improvement**: Emphasizing change management promotes a culture of adaptability and continuous improvement within the organization.

The Change Management Process

The change management process typically consists of several key steps:

1. **Change Identification**: Recognize the need for change based on feedback, stakeholder requests, or external factors. Document the proposed change clearly.
2. **Impact Assessment**: Analyze the potential impacts of the change on project objectives, resources, stakeholders, and processes. This may involve:
    - Conducting a SWOT analysis (Strengths, Weaknesses, Opportunities, Threats).
    - Gathering input from stakeholders to understand their perspectives and concerns.
3. **Change Proposal**: Develop a formal change proposal that outlines the nature of the change, its rationale, and expected benefits. Include details such as:
    - Affected stakeholders.

- Required resources and budget adjustments.
- Timeline for implementation.
4. **Stakeholder Engagement**: Communicate the proposed change to stakeholders and solicit their feedback. This step is critical for addressing concerns and building support for the change.
5. **Change Planning**: Create a comprehensive change management plan that includes:
    - **Communication Strategy**: Outline how information about the change will be disseminated to stakeholders.
    - **Training Plan**: Identify any training or support needed to help stakeholders adapt to the change.
    - **Risk Management Plan**: Assess potential risks associated with the change and develop mitigation strategies.
6. **Implementation**: Execute the change management plan, ensuring that all stakeholders are informed and engaged throughout the process. Key activities during this phase may include:
    - Conducting training sessions.
    - Providing resources and support.
    - Communicating progress updates.
7. **Monitoring and Evaluation**: Continuously monitor the implementation of the change to assess its effectiveness. This includes:

- Collecting feedback from stakeholders on their experiences with the change.
- Measuring the impact of the change against predefined success criteria.

8. **Reinforcement**: Once the change has been successfully implemented, reinforce the new processes or behaviors through ongoing support and communication. This can involve:
    - Celebrating successes and acknowledging contributions.
    - Providing ongoing training and resources as needed.

Key Strategies for Effective Change Management

1. **Create a Change Management Team**: Assemble a team of key stakeholders and change agents to lead and support the change initiative. This team should be responsible for planning, implementing, and monitoring the change.
2. **Communicate Effectively**: Maintain open lines of communication throughout the change process. Regular updates, meetings, and feedback sessions help keep stakeholders informed and engaged.
3. **Build a Change-Ready Culture**: Foster a culture that embraces change by encouraging innovation, adaptability, and open-mindedness among team members.

4. **Involve Stakeholders**: Engage stakeholders early in the change process to gather input, address concerns, and build support for the change initiative.
5. **Use Change Models**: Consider applying established change management models, such as Kotter's 8-Step Process for Leading Change or the ADKAR Model (Awareness, Desire, Knowledge, Ability, Reinforcement), to guide the change management process.
6. **Provide Training and Support**: Ensure that stakeholders receive the necessary training and support to adapt to the changes. Tailor training programs to address specific needs and concerns.
7. **Celebrate Milestones**: Recognize and celebrate milestones and successes throughout the change process to maintain motivation and reinforce commitment.
8. **Evaluate and Learn**: After implementing the change, conduct a post-implementation review to evaluate its effectiveness and identify lessons learned for future change initiatives.

Best Practices for Managing Change

1. **Be Proactive**: Anticipate potential changes and develop contingency plans to address them before they arise.

2. **Document Everything**: Keep detailed records of the change process, including proposals, communications, training materials, and feedback received. This documentation is valuable for future reference and improvement.
3. **Stay Flexible**: Be prepared to adapt the change management plan as necessary based on stakeholder feedback and the evolving project landscape.
4. **Lead by Example**: Leaders should model the desired behaviors and attitudes related to the change to encourage team members to follow suit.
5. **Ensure Alignment with Project Goals**: Always align change initiatives with overall project objectives and organizational goals to ensure that changes contribute positively to project success.

Conclusion

Change management is a crucial aspect of project management that helps ensure that necessary changes are implemented smoothly and effectively. By adopting a structured approach to change management, project managers can minimize resistance, enhance stakeholder engagement, and improve project outcomes. As we continue through this book, we will explore how change management integrates with other aspects of project management, such as risk management, quality control, and stakeholder engagement, to create a comprehensive approach to achieving successful project outcomes.

Chapter 13: Performance Measurement in Projects

Performance measurement is a vital aspect of project management that involves assessing and tracking the efficiency and effectiveness of project activities and outcomes. It enables project managers to determine whether a project is on track to meet its objectives, identify areas for improvement, and make informed decisions based on data. In this chapter, we will explore the importance of performance measurement, key metrics and techniques, and best practices for effectively measuring project performance.

Understanding Performance Measurement

Performance measurement refers to the process of collecting, analyzing, and reporting data related to project performance. It involves defining performance indicators, gathering relevant data, and interpreting the results to assess progress toward project goals.

Key Aspects of Performance Measurement:

1. **Establishing Performance Metrics**: Identifying and defining specific metrics that will be used to evaluate project performance.
2. **Data Collection**: Gathering data related to the defined performance metrics through various methods.

3. **Analysis and Interpretation**: Analyzing the collected data to determine performance levels and identify trends.
4. **Reporting**: Communicating performance results to stakeholders in a clear and concise manner.
5. **Continuous Improvement**: Using performance measurement data to inform decisions, improve processes, and enhance project outcomes.

Importance of Performance Measurement

1. **Informed Decision-Making**: Performance measurement provides project managers with data-driven insights that facilitate informed decision-making throughout the project lifecycle.
2. **Accountability and Transparency**: By measuring performance, project managers can hold team members accountable for their contributions and maintain transparency with stakeholders.
3. **Early Identification of Issues**: Regular performance measurement helps identify potential issues or deviations from the project plan early, allowing for timely corrective actions.
4. **Resource Optimization**: Performance metrics enable project managers to assess resource utilization and optimize the allocation of resources to enhance efficiency.
5. **Stakeholder Communication**: Performance measurement provides a basis for communicating progress and results to

stakeholders, helping to manage expectations and build trust.

Key Performance Metrics

Performance metrics are specific measures used to evaluate various aspects of project performance. Common categories of performance metrics include:

1. **Schedule Performance Metrics**:
     - **Planned Value (PV)**: The value of work planned to be completed by a specific time.
     - **Earned Value (EV)**: The value of work actually completed by a specific time.
     - **Actual Cost (AC)**: The actual cost incurred for the work completed by a specific time.
     - **Schedule Variance (SV)**: SV = EV - PV. This measures the difference between the earned value and the planned value.
     - **Schedule Performance Index (SPI)**: SPI = EV / PV. This ratio indicates schedule efficiency.
2. **Cost Performance Metrics**:
     - **Cost Variance (CV)**: CV = EV - AC. This measures the difference between the earned value and the actual cost.
     - **Cost Performance Index (CPI)**: CPI = EV / AC. This ratio indicates cost efficiency.

3. **Quality Performance Metrics**:
   - **Defect Rate**: The number of defects found in project deliverables relative to the total number of deliverables produced.
   - **Customer Satisfaction**: Measured through surveys or feedback from stakeholders regarding the quality of deliverables.
4. **Scope Performance Metrics**:
   - **Scope Change Rate**: The number of changes made to the project scope relative to the original scope.
   - **Scope Creep**: The unplanned expansion of project scope without adjustments to resources or timelines.
5. **Team Performance Metrics**:
   - **Team Velocity**: In agile projects, this measures the amount of work completed in a given iteration.
   - **Resource Utilization Rate**: The percentage of time team members are actively engaged in project tasks compared to their available work time.

Techniques for Performance Measurement

1. **Key Performance Indicators (KPIs)**: KPIs are quantifiable metrics that reflect critical success factors for a project. They should be specific,

measurable, achievable, relevant, and time-bound (SMART).
2. **Earned Value Management (EVM)**: EVM integrates scope, schedule, and cost metrics to provide a comprehensive view of project performance. It allows project managers to assess overall project health and make data-driven decisions.
3. **Regular Status Reports**: Creating and distributing regular status reports helps communicate performance results to stakeholders and keeps the project team informed of progress.
4. **Dashboards**: Utilizing project management dashboards can provide real-time visualizations of key performance metrics, making it easier to track performance at a glance.
5. **Benchmarking**: Comparing project performance against industry standards or best practices can provide insights into areas for improvement and highlight successful strategies.
6. **Surveys and Feedback**: Gathering feedback from stakeholders and team members through surveys can help assess satisfaction levels and identify areas for improvement.

Best Practices for Performance Measurement

1. **Define Clear Objectives**: Establish clear project objectives and ensure that performance metrics

align with these objectives to measure relevant outcomes.
2. **Select Relevant Metrics**: Choose performance metrics that provide meaningful insights into project success and align with stakeholder expectations.
3. **Regularly Review Performance**: Conduct regular performance reviews to assess progress, identify trends, and adjust strategies as needed.
4. **Involve the Team**: Engage team members in the performance measurement process to foster ownership and accountability for results.
5. **Communicate Results Transparently**: Share performance measurement results with stakeholders in a clear and transparent manner, highlighting successes and areas for improvement.
6. **Use Technology**: Leverage project management software and tools to streamline data collection, analysis, and reporting processes.
7. **Continuous Improvement**: Use performance measurement data to drive continuous improvement initiatives, refining processes and strategies to enhance future project performance.

Conclusion

Performance measurement is an essential component of effective project management that provides valuable insights into project performance, efficiency, and effectiveness. By establishing clear metrics, utilizing appropriate techniques, and implementing best practices, project managers can enhance decision-making, optimize resource allocation, and ultimately achieve project success. As we continue through this book, we will explore how performance measurement integrates with other aspects of project management, such as quality control, risk management, and change management, to create a comprehensive approach to delivering successful projects.

Chapter 14: Team Dynamics and Leadership in Projects

Team dynamics and leadership are crucial elements of successful project management. The effectiveness of a project team is often determined by how well team members interact, communicate, and collaborate. Strong leadership is essential to guide the team, foster a positive environment, and drive the project toward its objectives. In this chapter, we will explore the concepts of team dynamics, the role of leadership in project management, and strategies for building and maintaining effective project teams.

Understanding Team Dynamics

Team dynamics refer to the psychological and social processes that influence how team members interact and work together. These dynamics can significantly impact team performance, collaboration, and overall project success. Key factors influencing team dynamics include:

1. **Roles and Responsibilities**: Clear delineation of roles and responsibilities helps team members understand their contributions and how they fit into the larger project context. Role clarity fosters accountability and reduces confusion.

2. **Communication**: Open and effective communication is essential for team cohesion. Teams that communicate well are better equipped to resolve conflicts, share information, and collaborate effectively.
3. **Trust and Respect**: Trust among team members is foundational for successful collaboration. When team members trust each other, they are more likely to share ideas, take risks, and support one another.
4. **Conflict Resolution**: Conflict is a natural part of team dynamics. How conflicts are managed can either enhance team cohesion or lead to dysfunction. Effective conflict resolution strategies are essential for maintaining a positive team environment.
5. **Diversity**: Diverse teams bring a variety of perspectives, skills, and experiences, which can enhance creativity and problem-solving. However, diversity can also present challenges in communication and collaboration if not managed effectively.

The Role of Leadership in Project Management

Leadership plays a critical role in shaping team dynamics and driving project success. Effective project leaders inspire, motivate, and guide their teams through challenges while fostering an environment of collaboration and accountability. Key leadership styles relevant to project management include:

1. **Transformational Leadership**: Transformational leaders inspire and motivate team members by creating a vision and fostering a sense of purpose. They encourage innovation, support personal development, and create a positive team culture.
2. **Transactional Leadership**: This style focuses on structure, clear objectives, and rewards for achieving goals. Transactional leaders ensure that team members understand their roles and responsibilities and are held accountable for their performance.
3. **Servant Leadership**: Servant leaders prioritize the needs of their team members and empower them to succeed. This leadership style emphasizes collaboration, empathy, and active listening.
4. **Situational Leadership**: Effective leaders adapt their style to the needs of the team and the specific circumstances of the project. This flexibility allows leaders to provide the right level of support and direction based on team dynamics and project challenges.

Building and Maintaining Effective Project Teams

Creating and sustaining a high-performing project team involves several key strategies:

1. **Define Clear Goals and Objectives**: Clearly articulate project goals and objectives to ensure all team members are aligned and understand the project's purpose.
2. **Foster Open Communication**: Encourage open dialogue among team members. Implement regular check-ins, meetings, and feedback sessions to facilitate communication and address concerns.
3. **Establish Trust and Respect**: Build a culture of trust by promoting transparency, honesty, and respect among team members. Encourage collaboration and support to strengthen relationships.
4. **Promote Team Development**: Invest in team-building activities and training to enhance skills, improve collaboration, and foster a sense of belonging among team members.
5. **Encourage Diversity and Inclusion**: Embrace diversity by creating an inclusive environment where all team members feel valued and respected. Leverage diverse perspectives to enhance creativity and problem-solving.
6. **Set Clear Roles and Responsibilities**: Clearly define roles and responsibilities to ensure that

team members understand their contributions and how they relate to the project's overall objectives.
7. **Provide Support and Resources**: Ensure that team members have the necessary resources, tools, and support to perform their roles effectively. Address any barriers that may hinder their success.
8. **Implement Conflict Resolution Strategies**: Equip team members with tools and techniques for managing conflict constructively. Encourage open discussions to address disagreements and find common ground.
9. **Recognize and Celebrate Achievements**: Acknowledge individual and team accomplishments to boost morale and motivation. Celebrating successes fosters a positive team culture and encourages continued effort.
10. **Solicit Feedback and Adapt**: Regularly solicit feedback from team members to assess team dynamics and identify areas for improvement. Be open to adapting processes and approaches based on team input.

Challenges in Team Dynamics

Project teams may face several challenges that can negatively impact dynamics and performance:

1. **Communication Barriers**: Miscommunication or lack of communication can lead to misunderstandings and conflicts. Ensure that communication channels are clear and accessible.
2. **Resistance to Change**: Team members may resist changes in processes, roles, or project direction. Address concerns and involve team members in the change process to reduce resistance.
3. **Role Ambiguity**: Unclear roles can lead to confusion and conflict. Clearly define roles and responsibilities to avoid overlaps and gaps.
4. **Diverse Working Styles**: Team members may have different working styles and preferences, leading to potential friction. Encourage flexibility and adaptability among team members.
5. **Conflict**: Conflicts are natural but can disrupt team dynamics if not managed effectively. Implement conflict resolution strategies to address issues constructively.

Measuring Team Performance

To assess the effectiveness of team dynamics and leadership, consider the following metrics:

1. **Team Satisfaction Surveys**: Conduct regular surveys to gather feedback from team members

about their experiences, satisfaction, and perceptions of team dynamics.
2. **Performance Metrics**: Track project performance metrics such as adherence to schedule, budget compliance, and quality of deliverables to evaluate team effectiveness.
3. **Collaboration and Communication**: Assess the frequency and quality of communication among team members to gauge collaboration levels.
4. **Conflict Resolution Outcomes**: Monitor the outcomes of conflicts and the effectiveness of conflict resolution strategies to identify areas for improvement.
5. **Goal Achievement**: Measure progress toward project goals and objectives to evaluate overall team performance.

Conclusion

Team dynamics and leadership are critical components of successful project management. By fostering a positive team environment, promoting open communication, and employing effective leadership strategies, project managers can enhance team performance and drive project success. As we continue through this book, we will explore how team dynamics and leadership integrate with other aspects of project management, such as performance measurement, change management, and stakeholder engagement, to create a comprehensive approach to delivering successful projects.

Chapter 15: Conflict Resolution in Projects

Conflict is an inherent part of team dynamics and project management. While it can be challenging, effective conflict resolution is essential for maintaining team cohesion and ensuring project success. This chapter explores the nature of conflict in projects, common sources of conflict, conflict resolution techniques, and best practices for managing conflicts constructively.

Understanding Conflict in Projects

Conflict arises when team members have differing opinions, goals, values, or interests. In a project setting, conflict can manifest in various forms, including interpersonal disagreements, differing priorities, and competing resources. Recognizing the nature and sources of conflict is crucial for effective resolution.

Types of Conflict:

1. **Interpersonal Conflict**: Disagreements between individuals based on personal differences, communication styles, or interpersonal relationships.
2. **Task Conflict**: Disputes related to the work being done, such as differing views on project direction, priorities, or approaches.

3. **Role Conflict**: Confusion or disagreement about roles and responsibilities, which can lead to misunderstandings and friction.
4. **Resource Conflict**: Competition for limited resources, such as time, budget, or personnel, which can create tension among team members.

Common Sources of Conflict

Understanding the sources of conflict can help project managers anticipate and address issues proactively. Common sources of conflict in projects include:

1. **Communication Issues**: Miscommunication, lack of information, or differing communication styles can lead to misunderstandings and conflict.
2. **Diverging Goals**: Team members may have differing priorities or objectives, leading to conflicting interests.
3. **Role Ambiguity**: Unclear roles and responsibilities can create confusion and lead to disputes about who is responsible for what.
4. **Cultural Differences**: Diverse teams may have varying cultural norms and values, which can lead to misunderstandings and conflict.
5. **Stress and Pressure**: High-pressure environments, tight deadlines, and resource constraints can exacerbate tensions and lead to conflicts.

The Importance of Conflict Resolution

Effective conflict resolution is crucial for several reasons:

1. **Maintaining Team Cohesion**: Unresolved conflicts can lead to team fragmentation, decreased morale, and reduced collaboration.
2. **Enhancing Creativity**: Constructive conflict can foster innovation and creativity by encouraging diverse perspectives and ideas.
3. **Improving Decision-Making**: Resolving conflicts allows teams to make informed decisions that consider all viewpoints and potential solutions.
4. **Increasing Engagement**: When conflicts are managed well, team members are more likely to feel valued and engaged in the project.
5. **Promoting Continuous Improvement**: Effective conflict resolution contributes to a culture of open communication and continuous improvement within the team.

Conflict Resolution Techniques

Project managers can employ various techniques to resolve conflicts effectively. Here are some key approaches:

1. **Active Listening**: Encourage team members to listen actively to each other's perspectives. This involves understanding not just the words being

said, but also the emotions and motivations behind them.
2. **Open Communication**: Foster an environment where team members feel safe expressing their concerns and viewpoints. Encourage honest and respectful discussions.
3. **Identify Common Goals**: Help team members identify shared objectives and interests. Focusing on common goals can create a collaborative atmosphere for resolving conflicts.
4. **Mediation**: As a project manager or neutral third party, facilitate discussions between conflicting parties to help them reach a resolution. This may involve guiding them through the discussion and ensuring that each side is heard.
5. **Compromise**: Encourage parties to find a middle ground. Compromise involves each party giving up something to reach a mutually acceptable solution.
6. **Collaboration**: Encourage team members to work together to find creative solutions that satisfy everyone's needs. This approach fosters a sense of ownership and commitment to the outcome.
7. **Clarifying Roles and Responsibilities**: If role ambiguity is a source of conflict, clarify and document roles and responsibilities to reduce misunderstandings.
8. **Establishing Ground Rules**: Create ground rules for discussions to ensure respectful

communication and prevent escalation of conflicts.
9. **Seek External Support**: If conflicts become particularly challenging or unresolved, consider bringing in external mediators or facilitators to assist.

Steps in the Conflict Resolution Process

A structured approach to conflict resolution can enhance effectiveness. The following steps outline a typical conflict resolution process:

1. **Acknowledge the Conflict**: Recognize that a conflict exists and that it needs to be addressed. Avoiding or ignoring conflicts can lead to escalation.
2. **Gather Information**: Collect relevant information from all parties involved. Understand each person's perspective and the context of the conflict.
3. **Define the Issue**: Clearly articulate the nature of the conflict. Identify the underlying interests and needs of each party.
4. **Explore Solutions**: Encourage all parties to brainstorm potential solutions collaboratively. Evaluate each option for feasibility and acceptability.

5. **Agree on a Solution**: Reach a consensus on the most suitable solution. Ensure that all parties are committed to the agreed-upon resolution.
6. **Implement the Solution**: Put the solution into action. Assign responsibilities and establish timelines for implementation.
7. **Monitor the Outcome**: After implementing the solution, monitor the situation to ensure that the conflict has been resolved satisfactorily and that relationships remain positive.
8. **Learn from the Experience**: Reflect on the conflict resolution process to identify lessons learned. Consider how similar conflicts can be avoided or managed more effectively in the future.

Best Practices for Conflict Resolution

1. **Address Conflicts Early**: Proactively address conflicts as they arise to prevent escalation. Ignoring issues can lead to larger problems down the line.
2. **Maintain Professionalism**: Encourage a culture of professionalism where conflicts are resolved respectfully and constructively.
3. **Encourage Team Building**: Invest in team-building activities to strengthen relationships and foster a positive team culture, reducing the likelihood of conflicts.

4. **Foster Emotional Intelligence**: Promote emotional intelligence within the team to enhance understanding and empathy among team members.
5. **Lead by Example**: Model effective conflict resolution behaviors as a project manager. Demonstrate open communication, active listening, and respect for diverse perspectives.
6. **Document Agreements**: Document any agreements reached during the conflict resolution process to ensure clarity and accountability.
7. **Evaluate Conflict Resolution Processes**: Regularly assess the effectiveness of conflict resolution strategies and adjust them as needed to improve outcomes.

Conclusion

Conflict is a natural part of team dynamics in project management, but it can be effectively managed and resolved. By understanding the nature of conflict, employing appropriate resolution techniques, and following structured processes, project managers can foster a collaborative and productive team environment. In the following chapters, we will explore how effective conflict resolution integrates with other aspects of project management, such as team dynamics, leadership, and stakeholder engagement, to create a comprehensive approach to delivering successful projects.

Chapter 16: Documentation and Reporting in Projects

Effective documentation and reporting are essential components of project management that facilitate communication, enhance accountability, and ensure the successful execution of projects. This chapter explores the importance of documentation, types of project documents, best practices for creating effective documentation, and the role of reporting in project management.

The Importance of Documentation in Projects

Documentation serves as a foundational element in project management. It provides a structured approach to capturing project information, decisions, and processes. The benefits of effective documentation include:

1. **Clarity and Consistency**: Documentation helps ensure that all project stakeholders have a clear understanding of project objectives, processes, and expectations, reducing ambiguity and miscommunication.
2. **Knowledge Preservation**: Well-organized documentation preserves valuable knowledge and insights gained throughout the project,

facilitating knowledge transfer and continuity for future projects.
3. **Accountability**: Documentation establishes a record of decisions, actions, and responsibilities, fostering accountability among team members and stakeholders.
4. **Risk Management**: Thorough documentation aids in identifying and mitigating risks by providing a clear record of project plans, assumptions, and potential issues.
5. **Compliance and Auditing**: Many industries require compliance with regulatory standards. Documentation ensures that projects meet these standards and provides a basis for auditing.
6. **Stakeholder Communication**: Documentation serves as a communication tool that keeps stakeholders informed about project progress, changes, and decisions.

Types of Project Documents

Different types of documentation serve various purposes throughout the project lifecycle. Key project documents include:

1. **Project Charter**: A formal document that outlines the project's purpose, objectives, scope, stakeholders, and high-level requirements. It serves as the project's foundational reference.

2. **Project Plan**: A comprehensive document that details the project's scope, schedule, budget, resources, and risk management strategies. It serves as a roadmap for project execution.
3. **Requirements Documentation**: A record of stakeholder requirements and project specifications that guide project development and delivery.
4. **Risk Management Plan**: A document that identifies potential risks, their impact, and strategies for mitigation and response.
5. **Meeting Minutes**: A summary of discussions, decisions, and action items from project meetings. Meeting minutes help maintain a record of discussions and agreements.
6. **Progress Reports**: Regularly generated reports that provide updates on project status, including progress against objectives, milestones achieved, and any issues encountered.
7. **Change Requests**: Formal requests for changes to project scope, schedule, or resources, along with their rationale and impact analysis.
8. **Status Reports**: Periodic updates that summarize the current state of the project, including progress, challenges, and next steps.
9. **Final Project Report**: A comprehensive document that summarizes the entire project, including objectives, deliverables, lessons learned, and performance evaluations.

10. **Lessons Learned Documentation**: A record of insights gained during the project, highlighting what went well and areas for improvement.

Best Practices for Effective Documentation

To ensure that project documentation is effective and valuable, consider the following best practices:

1. **Be Clear and Concise**: Use clear language and avoid jargon. Aim for conciseness while providing enough detail to convey the necessary information.
2. **Use Standard Templates**: Utilize standardized templates for key documents to ensure consistency in format and content. This helps team members quickly understand and navigate the documents.
3. **Organize Documents Logically**: Structure documentation in a logical manner, using clear headings, subheadings, and sections to enhance readability and navigation.
4. **Version Control**: Implement version control for documents to track changes and maintain an accurate record of revisions. Clearly indicate the version number and date on each document.
5. **Engage Stakeholders**: Involve key stakeholders in the documentation process to ensure their input is captured and their perspectives are reflected in project documents.

6. **Regular Updates**: Keep documentation up to date throughout the project lifecycle. Regularly review and revise documents as needed to reflect changes in the project.
7. **Facilitate Accessibility**: Ensure that all team members and stakeholders have easy access to relevant documentation. Use collaborative platforms or document management systems for sharing.
8. **Encourage Feedback**: Create opportunities for team members and stakeholders to provide feedback on documentation. This can help identify gaps and improve clarity.
9. **Train Team Members**: Provide training on documentation practices and tools to ensure that team members understand the importance of documentation and how to create effective documents.
10. **Archive for Future Reference**: After project completion, archive documentation for future reference. This preserves valuable knowledge and insights for future projects.

The Role of Reporting in Project Management

Reporting is a critical aspect of project management that involves communicating project status, progress, and performance to stakeholders. Effective reporting keeps stakeholders informed, facilitates decision-making, and enhances accountability. Key components of reporting include:

1. **Types of Reports**:
    - **Status Reports**: Provide regular updates on project progress, including completed tasks, milestones achieved, and any issues or risks encountered.
    - **Progress Reports**: Focus on the overall progress of the project, highlighting accomplishments and areas requiring attention.
    - **Financial Reports**: Detail the project's financial performance, including budget utilization, expenditures, and forecasts.
2. **Frequency of Reporting**: Determine the appropriate frequency for reporting based on project complexity and stakeholder needs. Regular reporting helps maintain transparency and ensures timely communication.
3. **Tailoring Reports to Audiences**: Customize reports for different stakeholder groups. Executives may prefer high-level summaries, while team members may need more detailed information.
4. **Visual Aids**: Incorporate visual elements such as charts, graphs, and dashboards to enhance understanding and convey information more effectively.

5. **Highlighting Key Metrics**: Focus on key performance indicators (KPIs) that align with project objectives. Reporting on KPIs helps stakeholders assess project health and make informed decisions.
6. **Action Items and Next Steps**: Clearly outline action items, responsibilities, and next steps in reports. This ensures accountability and provides clarity on what is required moving forward.
7. **Feedback Mechanisms**: Include opportunities for stakeholders to provide feedback on reports. This can help identify areas for improvement and enhance future reporting practices.
8. **Use of Technology**: Leverage project management software and reporting tools to streamline reporting processes, automate data collection, and improve accuracy.

Conclusion

Effective documentation and reporting are essential for successful project management. By establishing clear documentation practices, maintaining up-to-date records, and implementing robust reporting processes, project managers can enhance communication, accountability, and overall project performance. As we continue through this book, we will explore how documentation and reporting integrate with other aspects of project management, such as stakeholder engagement, performance measurement, and risk management, to create a comprehensive approach to delivering successful projects.

Chapter 17: Tools and Technologies in Project Management

In today's fast-paced and increasingly complex project environments, leveraging the right tools and technologies is essential for effective project management. This chapter explores various tools and technologies available to project managers, their benefits, and how to select and implement the most appropriate solutions for your projects.

The Role of Tools and Technologies in Project Management

Tools and technologies facilitate project planning, execution, monitoring, and reporting. They enhance collaboration, streamline processes, and improve efficiency, ultimately leading to better project outcomes. Key benefits of using project management tools and technologies include:

1. **Improved Collaboration**: Tools enable team members to collaborate in real-time, regardless of location, fostering communication and teamwork.
2. **Enhanced Visibility**: Project management software provides dashboards and visualizations that offer insights into project progress, timelines, and resource allocation.

3. **Increased Efficiency**: Automation of repetitive tasks, such as scheduling and reporting, frees up time for project managers and team members to focus on more strategic activities.
4. **Better Resource Management**: Tools help track resource allocation, availability, and utilization, enabling project managers to make informed decisions.
5. **Data-Driven Decision Making**: Technologies allow for the collection and analysis of project data, providing insights that support better decision-making.
6. **Risk Management**: Many project management tools include features for identifying, assessing, and managing risks, enhancing project resilience.

Types of Project Management Tools

There are various categories of project management tools, each serving different aspects of the project lifecycle. Key types of tools include:

1. **Project Planning Tools**: These tools help project managers define project scope, develop schedules, and allocate resources. Examples include:
    - **Gantt Charts**: Visual representations of project timelines that illustrate task dependencies and durations (e.g., Microsoft Project, Smartsheet).

- **Work Breakdown Structure (WBS)**: Tools that help break down project deliverables into smaller, manageable components (e.g., WBS Schedule Pro).
2. **Collaboration and Communication Tools**: These tools enhance team collaboration and communication. Examples include:
    - **Instant Messaging Platforms**: Tools like Slack or Microsoft Teams facilitate quick communication among team members.
    - **Video Conferencing Tools**: Applications like Zoom or Google Meet support virtual meetings and discussions.
3. **Task and Workflow Management Tools**: These tools help manage tasks, assign responsibilities, and track progress. Examples include:
    - **Kanban Boards**: Visual task management boards that allow teams to organize and prioritize work (e.g., Trello, Asana).
    - **To-Do List Applications**: Simple task management tools for tracking individual tasks (e.g., Todoist, Microsoft To Do).
4. **Resource Management Tools**: Tools that assist in tracking and managing project resources. Examples include:
    - **Resource Allocation Software**: Applications that help plan and track resource usage (e.g., Resource Guru, 10,000ft).

- **Time Tracking Tools**: Tools for monitoring time spent on tasks and projects (e.g., Toggl, Harvest).
5. **Reporting and Analytics Tools**: These tools help generate reports and analyze project performance. Examples include:
    - **Business Intelligence Software**: Tools that provide insights through data visualization and analysis (e.g., Tableau, Power BI).
    - **Project Management Dashboards**: Customizable dashboards that display key project metrics and performance indicators.
6. **Risk Management Tools**: Tools specifically designed to identify, assess, and manage project risks. Examples include:
    - **Risk Assessment Matrices**: Tools that help visualize and prioritize risks based on likelihood and impact (e.g., RiskWatch).
    - **Risk Register Software**: Applications for tracking identified risks, mitigation strategies, and status (e.g., RiskyProject).
7. **Document Management Tools**: Tools for storing and managing project documents. Examples include:
    - **Cloud Storage Services**: Platforms that facilitate file sharing and collaboration (e.g., Google Drive, Dropbox).

- **Document Collaboration Tools**: Applications that allow multiple users to edit documents in real-time (e.g., Microsoft SharePoint, Confluence).

Selecting the Right Tools and Technologies

Choosing the right tools and technologies for project management is crucial for achieving project success. Consider the following factors when selecting tools:

1. **Project Complexity**: Assess the complexity of the project and the specific needs of the team. More complex projects may require advanced tools with robust features.
2. **Team Size and Distribution**: Consider the size of the team and whether team members are co-located or distributed. Collaboration tools may be essential for remote teams.
3. **Budget Constraints**: Evaluate the budget available for tools and technologies. Some tools offer free versions with limited features, while others may require significant investment.
4. **User-Friendliness**: Choose tools that are easy to use and require minimal training. User-friendly interfaces enhance adoption and efficiency.
5. **Integration Capabilities**: Assess whether the tools can integrate with existing systems and software used by the organization. Integration enhances efficiency and data accuracy.

6. **Scalability**: Consider whether the tools can scale with the organization's growth and evolving project management needs.
7. **Support and Training**: Look for vendors that provide adequate support, training resources, and documentation to help users effectively utilize the tools.
8. **Security and Compliance**: Ensure that the tools comply with relevant security standards and regulations, especially when handling sensitive project data.

Implementing Project Management Tools

Once the right tools have been selected, the next step is implementation. Effective implementation involves:

1. **Creating an Implementation Plan**: Develop a detailed plan outlining the steps required for tool implementation, including timelines, responsibilities, and milestones.
2. **Training Team Members**: Provide training sessions to ensure that all team members are familiar with the tools and can use them effectively.
3. **Encouraging Adoption**: Foster a culture of acceptance by encouraging team members to use the tools regularly and highlighting their benefits.

4. **Monitoring Usage and Feedback**: Regularly monitor tool usage and gather feedback from team members to identify any challenges or areas for improvement.
5. **Iterating and Improving**: Be open to making adjustments based on feedback and evolving project needs. Continuously seek opportunities to enhance tool effectiveness.

Future Trends in Project Management Tools

The landscape of project management tools is constantly evolving, driven by advancements in technology and changing project management practices. Key trends include:

1. **Artificial Intelligence (AI)**: AI-driven tools are emerging to automate routine tasks, analyze project data, and provide predictive analytics to enhance decision-making.
2. **Remote Collaboration Tools**: With the rise of remote work, tools that facilitate virtual collaboration, such as virtual whiteboards and online brainstorming platforms, are gaining popularity.
3. **Integration of Project Management with Other Business Functions**: Tools are increasingly integrating with other business systems, such as customer relationship management (CRM) and

enterprise resource planning (ERP), to enhance data flow and collaboration.
4. **Mobile Project Management**: Mobile applications are becoming more prevalent, allowing project managers and team members to access project information and communicate on the go.
5. **Focus on User Experience**: Vendors are prioritizing user experience in tool design, making them more intuitive and easier to use, thereby enhancing adoption rates.

Conclusion

Tools and technologies play a vital role in enhancing project management effectiveness. By selecting the right tools, implementing them effectively, and staying informed about emerging trends, project managers can improve collaboration, streamline processes, and achieve project success. As we continue through this book, we will explore how tools and technologies integrate with other aspects of project management, such as documentation, reporting, and stakeholder engagement, to create a comprehensive approach to delivering successful projects.

Chapter 18: Case Studies of Successful Projects

Case studies provide valuable insights into the practical application of project management principles and strategies. By examining successful projects, we can identify best practices, lessons learned, and innovative approaches that contributed to their success. This chapter presents several case studies across different industries, highlighting key factors that led to project success.

Case Study 1: Construction of the Burj Khalifa

Project Overview: The Burj Khalifa in Dubai, UAE, is the tallest building in the world, standing at 828 meters (2,717 feet). Completed in 2010, this architectural marvel is a symbol of modern engineering and design.

Key Success Factors:

1. **Thorough Planning**: The project began with meticulous planning, including a comprehensive feasibility study and design phase that accounted for various challenges, such as extreme weather conditions.
2. **Innovative Engineering Solutions**: The construction team employed innovative techniques, including a reinforced concrete core

and high-performance materials, to ensure structural stability and safety.
3. **Effective Resource Management**: The project utilized advanced scheduling software and resource allocation tools to optimize workforce productivity and manage a diverse range of materials and subcontractors.
4. **Strong Leadership**: Project leaders demonstrated exceptional leadership and communication skills, fostering collaboration among a multicultural workforce and aligning all stakeholders with the project vision.
5. **Stakeholder Engagement**: Continuous engagement with stakeholders, including government entities and local communities, helped to address concerns and maintain support throughout the project.

Results: The Burj Khalifa was completed on time and within budget, receiving accolades for its design and engineering. It has become a major tourist attraction and a significant economic driver for Dubai.

Case Study 2: NASA's Mars Rover Perseverance Mission

Project Overview: NASA's Mars Rover Perseverance was launched in July 2020 to explore the surface of Mars, conduct scientific research, and search for signs of ancient life. The mission aims to collect samples for potential future return to Earth.

Key Success Factors:

1. **Robust Project Planning**: The mission was meticulously planned, with clear objectives, timelines, and milestones established to guide the development of the rover and its scientific instruments.
2. **Cross-Disciplinary Collaboration**: Teams from various scientific and engineering disciplines collaborated closely, leveraging diverse expertise to solve complex challenges associated with space exploration.
3. **Innovative Technology**: The project incorporated cutting-edge technologies, including advanced robotics, artificial intelligence, and autonomous navigation systems, to enhance the rover's capabilities.
4. **Risk Management**: A proactive approach to risk management involved thorough testing of all systems and components before launch, as well as contingency plans to address potential issues during the mission.
5. **Public Engagement**: NASA actively engaged the public through educational programs and outreach initiatives, fostering excitement and support for the mission.

Results: Perseverance successfully landed on Mars in February 2021 and has since transmitted valuable data and images back to Earth, enhancing our understanding of the Martian environment and its potential for past life.

Case Study 3: The Launch of the iPhone

Project Overview: Apple's iPhone, first launched in 2007, revolutionized the smartphone industry and changed the way people interact with technology. The project involved extensive research, development, and marketing efforts.

Key Success Factors:

1. **Visionary Leadership**: Steve Jobs provided strong leadership and a clear vision for the iPhone, focusing on user experience and design, which guided the entire development process.
2. **Market Research and User-Centric Design**: Apple conducted extensive market research to understand user needs and preferences, resulting in a product that combined innovative technology with an intuitive interface.
3. **Cross-Functional Teams**: Collaboration among various teams, including hardware, software, and marketing, ensured alignment and facilitated rapid problem-solving during the development process.

4. **Effective Marketing Strategy**: Apple's marketing strategy emphasized the iPhone's unique features and capabilities, generating significant buzz and anticipation prior to launch.
5. **Agile Development Approach**: The project utilized an agile development approach, allowing for flexibility and quick adjustments in response to feedback and changing market conditions.

Results: The iPhone became a commercial success, setting the standard for smartphones and contributing significantly to Apple's growth and market dominance.

Case Study 4: The Renovation of the Louvre Museum

Project Overview: The Louvre Museum in Paris, France, underwent a significant renovation and expansion project, including the construction of the glass pyramid entrance, completed in 1989.

Key Success Factors:

1. **Clear Project Objectives**: The project aimed to modernize the museum while preserving its historical significance, resulting in a clear focus throughout the renovation process.
2. **Architectural Innovation**: The design of the glass pyramid, created by architect I.M. Pei, introduced a modern aesthetic while enhancing the museum's functionality and accessibility.

3. **Stakeholder Involvement**: The project involved extensive consultation with various stakeholders, including museum staff, local authorities, and the public, ensuring broad support and acceptance.
4. **Cultural Sensitivity**: The renovation was conducted with a deep respect for the museum's history and cultural significance, incorporating elements that honored its legacy.
5. **Phased Implementation**: The project was executed in phases to minimize disruption to museum operations and visitor access, allowing the museum to continue functioning during the renovation.

Results: The renovation was hailed as a success, transforming the Louvre into a modern cultural institution and attracting millions of visitors each year.

Case Study 5: Implementation of ERP Systems at Siemens

Project Overview: Siemens, a global engineering and technology company, implemented an enterprise resource planning (ERP) system to streamline its operations and improve efficiency across various business units.

Key Success Factors:

1. **Comprehensive Needs Assessment**: Siemens conducted a thorough assessment of its operational needs and challenges, ensuring that the selected ERP system aligned with business objectives.
2. **Change Management**: A robust change management strategy was developed to prepare employees for the transition, including training programs and ongoing support.
3. **Executive Sponsorship**: Strong support from top executives helped secure buy-in from stakeholders and emphasized the project's importance across the organization.
4. **Cross-Functional Collaboration**: Teams from different departments collaborated closely during the implementation, fostering a sense of ownership and shared purpose.
5. **Continuous Improvement**: Siemens established a framework for continuous improvement, allowing for ongoing evaluation and optimization of the ERP system post-implementation.

Results: The ERP implementation resulted in improved operational efficiency, reduced costs, and enhanced data visibility across the organization, positioning Siemens for greater competitiveness in the market.

Conclusion

These case studies illustrate the diverse applications of project management principles across various industries. Each project demonstrates the importance of thorough planning, effective communication, stakeholder engagement, and innovative problem-solving. By learning from these successful projects, project managers can apply best practices and strategies to enhance their own project outcomes, ultimately contributing to organizational success. As we move forward in this book, we will explore additional topics and techniques that can further empower project managers in their quest for excellence.

Chapter 19: Future Trends in Project Management

As the landscape of business and technology evolves, project management continues to adapt to new challenges and opportunities. Understanding future trends in project management is crucial for professionals seeking to remain competitive and effective in their roles. This chapter explores the emerging trends shaping the future of project management, highlighting innovations, methodologies, and practices that will define the profession in the coming years.

1. Increased Adoption of Agile Methodologies

Overview: Agile methodologies have gained significant traction across various industries, moving beyond software development to influence project management in sectors such as healthcare, marketing, and construction.

Key Points:

- **Flexibility and Responsiveness**: Agile emphasizes iterative development, allowing teams to respond quickly to changing requirements and stakeholder feedback.
- **Cross-Functional Teams**: Agile promotes collaboration among diverse team members,

breaking down silos and fostering a culture of innovation.
- **Focus on Customer Value**: Agile methodologies prioritize delivering value to customers through continuous improvement and regular feedback loops.

Impact: The shift towards Agile will encourage project managers to adopt more flexible approaches, enabling them to navigate uncertainty and deliver projects that align with evolving stakeholder needs.

2. Integration of Artificial Intelligence (AI) and Automation

Overview: The integration of AI and automation into project management tools is transforming how projects are planned, executed, and monitored.

Key Points:

- **Automated Task Management**: AI-powered tools can automate repetitive tasks, such as scheduling and reporting, allowing project managers to focus on higher-level strategic activities.
- **Predictive Analytics**: AI can analyze historical project data to provide insights and forecasts, helping managers anticipate potential risks and challenges.

- **Enhanced Decision-Making**: AI tools can support decision-making by offering data-driven recommendations based on real-time analysis.

Impact: The use of AI and automation will increase efficiency and accuracy in project management, allowing teams to deliver projects more effectively and with fewer errors.

3. Focus on Sustainability and Social Responsibility

Overview: As organizations prioritize sustainability and corporate social responsibility (CSR), project management practices are evolving to incorporate these principles.

Key Points:

- **Sustainable Project Planning**: Project managers are increasingly required to consider environmental and social impacts when planning and executing projects.
- **Green Project Management**: Techniques such as life cycle assessment and sustainable resource allocation are becoming essential in project planning.
- **Stakeholder Engagement**: Engaging stakeholders around sustainability goals fosters collaboration and support for environmentally responsible initiatives.

Impact: The emphasis on sustainability will require project managers to develop new skills and strategies to balance project objectives with environmental and social considerations.

4. Remote and Hybrid Work Environments

Overview: The COVID-19 pandemic has accelerated the shift toward remote and hybrid work models, fundamentally changing how teams collaborate on projects.

Key Points:

- **Virtual Collaboration Tools**: The adoption of digital collaboration tools, such as video conferencing and project management software, has become essential for remote teams.
- **Flexible Work Arrangements**: Project managers must navigate the challenges and benefits of flexible work arrangements, fostering team cohesion despite geographical distances.
- **Employee Well-being**: Prioritizing employee well-being and work-life balance is critical in maintaining team morale and productivity in remote settings.

Impact: Project managers will need to develop new leadership and communication strategies to effectively manage distributed teams and maintain engagement and accountability.

5. Emphasis on Continuous Learning and Development

Overview: The rapidly changing project management landscape necessitates a commitment to continuous learning and professional development.

Key Points:

- **Skill Development**: Project managers must continuously upgrade their skills to keep pace with emerging trends, technologies, and methodologies.
- **Certification Programs**: The demand for specialized certifications, such as Agile, Scrum, and AI in project management, is expected to grow.
- **Knowledge Sharing**: Encouraging a culture of knowledge sharing and mentorship within organizations can enhance overall project management capabilities.

Impact: A focus on continuous learning will empower project managers to adapt to new challenges and leverage innovative approaches, ultimately enhancing project outcomes.

6. Enhanced Use of Data Analytics

Overview: Data analytics is becoming increasingly important in project management, providing insights that inform decision-making and improve project performance.

Key Points:

- **Data-Driven Decision Making**: Project managers are leveraging data analytics to evaluate project performance, identify trends, and optimize resource allocation.
- **Real-Time Monitoring**: Advanced analytics tools enable real-time monitoring of project metrics, allowing for timely adjustments and proactive risk management.
- **Performance Benchmarking**: Analyzing data from previous projects helps establish benchmarks for success, guiding future project planning and execution.

Impact: The integration of data analytics will enhance project visibility and enable project managers to make informed, strategic decisions based on empirical evidence.

7. Focus on Emotional Intelligence (EQ)

Overview: Emotional intelligence is increasingly recognized as a vital competency for effective project management, particularly in fostering collaboration and managing team dynamics.

Key Points:

- **Empathy and Communication**: Project managers with high emotional intelligence can better understand and address the needs and concerns of team members and stakeholders.
- **Conflict Resolution**: Emotional intelligence facilitates effective conflict resolution by promoting understanding and collaboration among team members.
- **Leadership and Motivation**: Leaders with strong EQ can inspire and motivate their teams, enhancing overall performance and engagement.

Impact: The emphasis on emotional intelligence will lead to more effective leadership practices, resulting in improved team dynamics and project outcomes.

8. Increased Use of Cloud-Based Project Management Solutions

Overview: Cloud-based project management tools are becoming the norm, enabling teams to collaborate and manage projects from anywhere.

Key Points:

- **Accessibility and Flexibility**: Cloud solutions allow team members to access project

information and collaborate in real time, regardless of their location.
- **Scalability**: Cloud-based tools can easily scale to accommodate projects of varying sizes and complexity, making them suitable for organizations of all types.
- **Integration Capabilities**: Many cloud solutions offer integration with other software applications, streamlining workflows and enhancing efficiency.

Impact: The widespread adoption of cloud-based solutions will facilitate greater collaboration and efficiency in project management, enabling teams to respond quickly to changing circumstances.

Conclusion

The future of project management is poised for transformation, driven by technological advancements, changing workforce dynamics, and an increased focus on sustainability and social responsibility. By staying informed about these trends and embracing new methodologies, tools, and practices, project managers can enhance their effectiveness and contribute to the success of their organizations. As we conclude this book, remember that the ability to adapt to change and embrace innovation will be key to thriving in the ever-evolving landscape of project management.

Chapter 20: Conclusion: The Art of Balancing

As we reach the conclusion of this exploration into project management, it's clear that the art of balancing—between time, budget, and resources—is at the heart of successful project execution. This balance is not merely a matter of keeping everything in check; it requires a strategic approach, keen insights, and an ability to adapt to the ever-changing landscape of project demands.

The Essence of Balance in Project Management

Balancing the three constraints—time, budget, and resources—serves as the foundational framework for effective project management. Each constraint influences the others, and any shift in one can have significant repercussions on the others. For instance, compressing timelines often leads to increased costs or the need for additional resources, while budget cuts may necessitate an extended schedule or reduced scope.

Key Insights on Balancing:

- **Dynamic Interplay**: Recognize that these constraints are interrelated. A successful project manager must continuously evaluate and adjust

their strategies based on the evolving project landscape.
- **Prioritization**: Understand the project's goals and prioritize the constraints accordingly. For some projects, timely delivery might be paramount, while for others, staying within budget or maintaining quality might take precedence.
- **Flexibility and Adaptability**: A successful project manager must remain flexible, willing to pivot strategies as circumstances change. This agility enables teams to respond to unexpected challenges without derailing the project.

Embracing Best Practices

Throughout this book, we've discussed numerous best practices that contribute to achieving this delicate balance. From establishing clear project scopes and engaging stakeholders effectively to leveraging the right tools and technologies, each practice plays a vital role in managing projects successfully.

1. **Stakeholder Engagement**: Involving stakeholders from the outset fosters alignment and reduces the likelihood of scope creep. Regular communication helps to manage expectations and encourages collaborative problem-solving.

2. **Thorough Planning**: Detailed planning lays the groundwork for project success. This includes defining project scope, establishing timelines, and accurately forecasting budgets. Effective planning provides a roadmap that guides teams through the project lifecycle.
3. **Continuous Monitoring and Evaluation**: Regularly reviewing project progress against established metrics allows project managers to identify potential issues early and make informed decisions. This proactive approach is essential for maintaining balance throughout the project.
4. **Risk Management**: Identifying and mitigating risks is crucial for keeping projects on track. A robust risk management plan ensures that potential disruptions are anticipated and addressed before they escalate into significant challenges.
5. **Team Dynamics and Leadership**: Fostering a collaborative team environment enhances communication, creativity, and problem-solving. Strong leadership inspires team members to stay engaged and committed to achieving project objectives.

Looking Ahead: The Future of Project Management

As we look to the future, project management will continue to evolve. Emerging trends such as the integration of artificial intelligence, the focus on sustainability, and the shift toward remote collaboration will shape how projects are managed.

Project managers will need to stay abreast of these developments and be prepared to adopt new methodologies and tools that enhance their ability to balance the constraints effectively. Continuous learning and professional development will be essential for project managers seeking to navigate the complexities of modern project environments.

Final Thoughts

Ultimately, the art of balancing time, budget, and resources in project management is about creating value—delivering successful outcomes that meet or exceed stakeholder expectations while fostering a positive team environment. It requires a blend of strategic thinking, emotional intelligence, and a commitment to excellence.

As you move forward in your project management journey, remember that achieving balance is an ongoing process, one that requires vigilance, adaptability, and a focus on the big picture. Embrace the challenges that come with project management, and let the art of balancing be your guiding principle, leading you to successful projects and impactful results.

Thank you for joining me on this exploration of project management. May your future projects be characterized by balance, collaboration and success.

www.ingramcontent.com/pod-product-compliance
Lightning Source LLC
Chambersburg PA
CBHW062106220526
45471CB00010B/3628